GW00982572

ROUND THE SQUARE
& UP THE TOWER
CLIFFORD CHAMBERS, WARWICKSHIRE

'I like this place, and willingly could waste my time in it'.
William Shakespeare, Celia, *As You Like It*, 2.6.93-4

This book is dedicated to the people and creatures who have lived here for over one thousand years and left no record except the perpetuation of this pleasant place.

Female and male heads, corbel terminals on the south exterior wall of St Helen's church

Commissioned, conducted and published by the Hosking Houses Trust
© HHT 2013
Designed by Oliver Hutton and Paula Dyer
Printed by W&G BAIRD Ltd
ISBN 978-0-9573142-2-1

hosking
houses
trust

Research, writing and editorial team

Sally Abell contributed local research and interviews having lived in the village for twenty years and raised her family here. She read history at York University and has extensive journalistic experience, locally and nationally. She works for the Women's Farm and Garden Association and together with Sarah Hosking edits the village newsletter.

Nat Alcock contributed the architectural study of the buildings in the Square. He is an Emeritus Reader at Warwick University and has undertaken building research for the Shakespeare Birthplace Trust, the National Trust and English Heritage. He is a member of the Society of Antiquaries and was president of the Vernacular Architecture Group.

Stefan Buczacki contributed the chapter on the River Stour. The author of over fifty books on natural history and biography, he is a Fellow of the Linnean Society, holds an honorary chair at Liverpool John Moores University and has an honorary doctorate from Derby University. A well-known broadcaster, he lives in the village and chairs the Parish Council.

John Cheal worked for ten months on photography in the village. He has, since his retirement, developed his specialism of photography while working at Holy Trinity Church, Stratford-upon-Avon as church warden and verger. He has researched and compiled books on the glass and misericords, and illustrated the major study by Val Horsler *Shakespeare's Church: a parish for the world.*

Paul Edmondson (chair of HHT) is Head of Research and Knowledge at the Shakespeare Birthplace Trust and Director of the Stratford Poetry Festival. He lectures internationally on Shakespeare and has published several articles and books. He is also an ordained priest of the Church of England.

Val Horsler contributed research on the church and churchyard and has initially edited throughout. She worked for over thirty years in archaeological publishing for the Council of British Archaeology and English Heritage. She has published with the National Archives and Third Millenium Information and is a member of the Society of Antiquaries.

Sarah Hosking instigated the book and has written otherwise unattributed sections. She trained as an artist and had a career of fifty years in arts administration, exhibition organisation and arts business studies. She worked for the NHS as designer and co-authored *Healing the Hospital Environment* (1999) about hospital premises. She founded HHT on her retirement in 2000.

Roger Pringle contributed the chapter about Michael Drayton. He was formerly director of the Shakespeare Birthplace Trust. His books include poetry and he directed the Stratford Poetry Festival for many years. He has honorary degrees from Birmingham City and Coventry Universities, he is a trustee of the Shakespeare Birthplace Trust and an honorary governor of the Royal Shakespeare Theatre.

About the Hosking Houses Trust (charity no 1076713)

Active since 2002, the Trust offers residencies in Church Cottage, no.35, the Square. These are available to women writers over the age of forty, of established merit who need a period of financially protected domestic peace in which to start, continue or complete innovative work about any subject; residencies are usually between three weeks and three months. The Trust is run by the secretary/founder and six trustees. This book is in support of their work.
sarahhosking@btinternet.com
www.hoskinghouses.co.uk

Contents

⊙ Illustrations

Period photographs in the text (unless otherwise attributed) are from the Pippet archive: Warwickshire County Record Office and contemporary photographs (unless otherwise attributed) are by John Cheal. Some further unattributed photographs occur in the text for design purposes.

The drawn plan of the Square and the collaged cut-paper map of the River Stour are prepared by Sarah Hosking.

Each chapter has a small picture-symbol: these are captioned where required.

Choir and congregation processing past the the old dairy, 1950s
Village archive

Foreword

When I was asked to be patron of this book, I was still Editor of *The Archers*.
The publication of *Around the Square and Up the Tower* coincides with my retirement from the programme after twenty-two years of very active service.
What is it about a village and its residents that, in fact and fiction, remains so appealing?

The Archers, remember, started in 1950 as a one-week trial-run over Whitsun in the Midlands area only. It was so popular that in 1951 the BBC aired it nationally for a further three months and simply never stopped as listening figures grew and grew. It was and is about a farming family and their community. But in those early days it was also a vehicle for informing farmers about innovations in farming as the nation had to feed itself after the austerity of the war years. Handily, the general public could also be encouraged to be aware of country matters such as closing gates, not washing their hands in the water trough and not smoking against a haystack.

Since those innocent times, *The Archers*, through character and drama, has presented many issues of contemporary interest. These include organic versus conventional farming, genetically modified crops, animal torture, abortion, divorces (several), sudden death (a few), lingering dementia at 'The Laurels', love in every permutation (straight, gay, lasting, fleeting, hopeless, stupid, pure), racism, many attacks and robberies, epilepsy, cancer, addiction (gambling, drugs, drink), prison (several times), family splits, homelessness and disability.

Clifford Chambers, unlike Ambridge, is of course a real place (hush my mouth!). While producers and editors of drama can choose and select, cut and paste, Clifford Chambers moves on through time, as it were, 'organically' and mostly, save occasional political interference, without prescription. It has not experienced much violence; there was a riot (I gather from this book), in 1529 and a carpet was stolen from the church and a clock from a house in the late 1990s, a few car aerials have been broken and paint stripper thrown at a car. In recent years, as in many villages, agricultural issues have taken a back seat and there are far fewer farm workers now living in the area.

Reality is a funny business. There are villages like Ambridge with an active church, pub and shop with the leadership that keeps such enterprises running but there are many that are not like that. Part of the appeal of *The Archers* is that it represents an ideal of community life as well as a place sometimes of adventure and turmoil. High drama side by side with the everyday.

The reality of Clifford Chambers today is that it is also hugely influenced by drama. Stratford-upon-Avon, separated by a lovely country path across the fields and over the River Stour, is under two miles away. Stratford is culturally so extraordinary that it significantly affects the nearby villages in a way that Borchester hasn't a hope of affecting Ambridge. Stratford is similar to a small university town with a proportion of the population that is seasonal (tourists) and temporary (theatre people and students). Many people live in Stratford and spread out into the nearby villages like Clifford Chambers, attracted by the blend of heritage, creativity and learning as well as the beauty of the Warwickshire countryside. And indeed Clifford Chambers is a beautiful place in which to live or to visit.

This delightful book, choc-a-block full of insight, information and charm is yours to enjoy. ◎◎

Vanessa Whitburn
Stratford-upon-Avon 2013

Introduction

I have over the years collected many church guides and village histories. They are often the result of experienced people retiring to the countryside and bringing their professionalism with them. All are inspired by affection for a place, and they contain good and sometimes original research.

However, none that I have found are an attractive bedtime read or consider aspects of urbanisation in a village or the future of churches redundant for the purpose of worship, and they tend to look backwards and not forwards. These are issues that I introduce and consider albeit briefly, because they are important and pertain closely to this village.

This book has been written partly for people who may not usually read history books, but who might enjoy this one. I have also written it for people who do read history books and who may conclude that this sort of book is one way of encouraging new readers to enjoy the subject. History is a tricky customer and has been defined as 'one damned thing after another', but it is also determined by how we regard it. We often make the past look a lot prettier than it really was, and most television historical dramas do not help in this respect. Part of our job is to de-prettify where necessary.

Clifford Chambers is described in the Domesday Book (started in 1085) and the church is also written up in the Pevsner architectural guides. My co-authors and I have studied the Church of St Helen and its graveyard, as well as the Square and its houses, the land and Duck Lane running to the River Stour, and the river itself. We include reminiscences from the people who have lived here up to recent times. We consider how the past has shaped the present and how we respond to this environment today. We hope that we have presented some serious issues but not in a solemn way.

Clifford Chambers is a cul-de-sac village and its only road (apart from a short feed road, three closes and another minor private road) ends at the manor. The history of that fine building is another story, so we merely refer to it in passing as we do to the splendid fifteenth-century rectory by the church which has an architecture and a past so complex that we have omitted it in the aim of keeping our subject manageable.

Any serious historian will be aware of how many omissions there are in this book. We have not considered where the money was sourced to build, rebuild and alter the church, nor the type of authority that operated here over many decades, nor how local and national government impacted on the place. The Norman conquest, the Reformation, the Reform bills and women's emancipation, industrial and agrarian revolutions, education and public health acts, the world wars and the welfare state before the recent technological revolution are only mentioned when they directly affected the lives of people here.

Remembrance Sunday, 1972
Village archive

A village is a geographical and demographic unit that is larger than a hamlet and smaller than a town. While thousands of villages have developed organically over the centuries as small, rural settlements, there are other sorts of village. These include deliberately created estate villages and villages built as picturesque follies, as well as utopian villages, industrial villages and twentieth-century philanthropic villages.

The village can also exist as a dream of utopia and our village is such a one. Its single, winding street, possibly delineated by wandering cattle vaguely grazing and now lined with timber-framed cottages, is protected from fringe development partly by the pattern of landowning and also because much of the village is susceptible to floods. Now advertised as being on Shakespeare's Way, it has attracted urban seekers after poetic calm who have superimposed their urban requirements on pastoral simplicity with mixed results. Life here in previous times was physically hard and constrained in opportunities, but modernisation has come at some cost. This is the subject of our small book; the history is included to explore the lineage of the place and establish its value.

The book has been put together primarily for the people who already know the place but also for people elsewhere, perhaps living in similar locations who will look around and perhaps perceive them afresh.

Seven people have produced this book and what with collaborating, interfering with each others' work and editing, 'we' has become the easiest way to identify 'the author'. If the first person is used, the writer is identified. Our data will be found under 'Research, writing and editorial team' on page 2.

Among our small team we have established academics with a string of qualifications, so we have ample experience of producing academic texts and of obeying the rules of research and presentation. However, we have deliberately avoided such an approach because we wanted to produce a book that could be enjoyed in part or in total equally by a child wanting to look at the pictures and by an interested adult. This intention has dictated our style in general, but the styles of the three separate, contributed chapters are those of the writers concerned.

But there has remained the problem in making a readable book out of the work delivered by several contributors, all of whom are exhaustively thorough and passionate about their specialism. Ultimately, we simply could not include all the data assembled from (for example) the parish records from 1538, nor about the many ceilings of chamfered beams, nor the name of the man who used to drive the bus carrying people to evensong from Stratford, nor when the second and third church clock faces were installed, nor how many cats the RSPCA found at no.35. Nothing has been wasted however, as our Internet website is the ideal medium to carry all such extra material in total and unaltered. It is the place where enthusiasts can browse unimpeded.

We fully understand the value and significance of references and footnotes in academic work. Both Dr Nat Alcock and Dr Roger Pringle supplied these to accompany their chapters, but when we came to compiling these and all the other accumulated material into a narrative, we felt that the academic data got in the way of our intention.

We therefore decided to include the full, unedited script of these two excellent chapters on the Hosking Houses Trust website. This also includes material from Nat Alcock about the family relationships and ownership of the individual houses in the Square up to 1951, which read as the excellent original research that they are, but which were over-detailed as part of the final narrative text. We also include material researched by Val Horsler on the village's parish records, and data from the survey of the graveyard and church monuments, linking them to family histories.

Between the seven of us we could have compiled a bibliography that would have been as lengthy as it was cumbersome and would have looked like showing off. Therefore, we are here indicating a few books that have been salient in this project:

Recommended books
Roy Strong's *A Little History of the English Country Church* (Vintage 2008) is exemplary and charming to read. Regarding the Reformation, Eamon Duffy's magisterial study *The Stripping of the Altars* (Yale University Press 1992) is revelatory, as is everything else he has written.

Some village studies have become classics and Ronald Blythe's *Akenfield, Portrait of an English Village* (Allen Lane 1969) holds the prize, but needs to be read with its worthy companion by Craig Taylor, *Return to Akenfield, Portrait of a Village in the 21st century* (Granta Books 2006).

The Dillon, edited by Angela Hewins (Elm Tree Books 1981), is a wonderful read about a Stratford man, while the classic novel that is thinly disguised autobiography about rural working class life is Flora Thompson's *Lark Rise to Candleford* (Oxford University Press 1939).

We were inspired to commission a study of the river by Olivia Laing's book, *To The River* (Canongate Books 2011). For all plant and ecological matters we recommend Richard Mabey's *Weeds* (Profile Books 2012), which handles complex biological issues with cultural learning.

The fiction that has best fuelled us is Evelyn Waugh's *Helena* (Chapman and Hall 1951) which is a fantasy about the woman who became venerated as St Helen but who was historically the mother of the Emperor Constantine. In 2012, we invited the Trust's patron, Marina Warner, to come and give a talk about this woman who exists on the edge of fact and fiction, in the church of St Helen in our village. The evening was enchanting and she too referred to Waugh's novel that captures the spirit of her life, even though the facts have largely disappeared.

Pictures

'What is the use of a book without pictures?' cried Alice in *Alice in Wonderland*.

We agree and so have included as many as we can afford and as varied as we can find. The nature of photography itself is enormously fluid, and we have used four main picture sources. The Revd Pippet was rector here from 1895 until 1918 and took dozens of photographs that are preserved on glass negatives. We then commissioned John Cheal, a photographer whose approach we liked, to photograph our part of the village for eight months. Our third source is people's personal photographs and our fourth is a miscellany of pictures of all sorts as they came to our notice and which we felt compelled to include.

In a section entitled 'History according to 'A'' we have selected twenty-five words, mainly nouns but some adjectives, and matched them with pictures and text to illustrate twethy-five examples of historical 'somethings' which we regard as significant in one way or another. From' Abnormality' to 'Attention', they all relate to the immediate area and it has been our method of fitting a lot of perhaps peripheral information into a simple format that has been fun to compile and, we hope, will be entertaining to read.

In unravelling local history, names can be helpful or a distraction. Monk's Barn Farm nearby is a beguiling name but there is no actual evidence that the village or the farm ever had monks. Duck Lane was first documented in 1910 but according to those who lived there during the 1950/60s, the name had fallen out of use until the 1990s when it was rediscovered. There are ducks on the river here, and anecdote says they used to be decapitated and hung from washing lines to bleed before plucking, but how hungry would we be before we ate Donald? Those of us who remember a wartime childhood will know the answer, and it is the difficulty of discerning history from habit and wishful thinking that we try to explore.
ⓔⓔ

Sarah Hosking
33, Duck Lane
The Square
Clifford Chambers
Stratford-upon-Avon
Warwickshire
CV37 8HT

sarahhosking@btinternet.com
July 2013

The bell outside no.32, Duck Lane

The assorted doors of the houses in the Square and nearby vary from being locked and unused to clean and painted. These are some of them

The Place

On first hearing the name of Clifford Chambers, some people think they are looking for a set of solicitors' offices in Stratford. We shall explain the reasons for its strange name in due course but we first need to describe it.

The village is within two miles of Stratford's south-east side. It was in the county of Gloucestershire until 1931, when the boundaries were altered and it became Warwickshire's most southern tip, and the church remained in the diocese of Gloucester until 2003.

The parish of Clifford Chambers and Milcote is a strange shape (see the map under Agriculture in the 'A' section); it has 404 people on the register of electors (this does not include children), occupying 255 residential properties (2012/13 figures) most of whose occupants are aged over forty-five. Its history is uneventful and only two mildly famous people have ever lived here. The village today has a pub and a church but no shop or school and everyone goes elsewhere for nearly everything.

Clifford Chambers nearly had a very different recent history. In June 1925, a large black limousine was seen being driven slowly through the village towards the manor which was its destination. The couple inside were Mr and Mrs Elmhirst, and Dorothy Elmhirst was one of America's wealthiest heiresses and used her position extensively to philanthropic and cultural ends. Born Dorothy Whitney and the widow of Willard Straight, she was a passionate Shakespeare scholar and had visited his tomb that morning.

She was in England on a mission to find a property they could buy and develop as a centre for arts and culture, offering education and performance, commissioning and patronage to the highest level. The manor in Clifford Chambers with its extensive properties, river frontage, ravishing seclusion and yet proximity to Stratford seemed ideal. It was tentatively on the market, being then owned by Mrs Kathleen Douty who had been widowed in 1911. However, fate immediately intervened when Mrs Douty suddenly met and married the tall and dashing Colonel Rees-Mogg and withdrew the manor from sale. They then both lived there until their deaths in 1949.

Dorothy Whitney Elmhirst contained her disappointment and went to Devon where she and her husband bought and endowed Dartington Hall which came to fulfil her ambitions as a national cultural centre. There is an odd postscript to this.

In 2002, the Hosking Houses Trust acquired the tiniest cottage in the Square, no.35 and set it up as a residence for women writers. In 2010, the writer/biographer Jane Brown applied for a residency having been commissioned by Dorothy Whitney Elmhirst's youngest but by now elderly son to write his mother's biography. She was aware of the diary entry about this 1925 visit and was struck by the serendipitous opportunity to stay in the same village near the Manor House that had so nearly become a major cultural centre.

We have included this odd incident because this is not a conventional village history but includes incidents (such as this one), also items and pictures that help identify the place. In pursuit of this, we commissioned four historical studies; three of them cover the church, the River Stour and the area next to the church called the Square; the fourth is a study of the Tudor poet Michael Drayton who spent a lot of time here in the sixteenth and early seventeenth centuries, and whose muse, whom he called his 'Idea', Anne Rainsford, is commemorated in the church. The whole is put together with comments and pictures.

We undertook this book because we wanted to explore the history of the Square, assuming it was the oldest part of the village. It looks medieval with its wonky half-timbered cottages and the evocatively named Duck Lane leading to what anecdote holds was the ford in the river, with the pre-Norman church. Whatever the weather, it looks adorable; so it stands to reason it must be old. It may stand to reason but it does not stand up to scrutiny.

Research has shown that it is not the oldest part of the village. Its Tudorbethan appearance belies reality and affects how we look at it. But the consequence of this mistake was that we felt it even more incumbent upon us to discover some of the accurate history of the place, not least because it epitomises a particular rural dream. This place is an estate agent's ideal, a fantasy of old England serving the great god nostalgia. With its half-timbered cottages beside a church above a winding river, gardens and meandering paths with blossom and birdsong, the Square is what estate agents call a highly desirable property opportunity.

Shakespeare-land is the name popularly given to this part of the Midlands. Situated on the edge of the Cotswolds, with Warwick and Kenilworth nearby with their castles, Stratford and the villages around epitomise the romantic vision of timber-framed cottages, hollyhocks, Tudor poets, village greens and medieval churches. The properties in such locations are highly desirable; but do we who live here really understand the reality of these delightful surroundings? Or is the image of the place, touted on hundreds of placemats and tourist leaflets, an over-idealised chimera? This rural dream is epitomised by our small village; so we decided to analyse its appeal. Is what we look at a visionary sham or do we understand its reality? Do we care for it by perpetuation or by damage or by development or by a bit of everything?

Above all towers what Fay Weldon calls Castle Shakespeare, who strangely sanctifies this place and the three theatres in nearby Stratford built in his honour. Commemorated in pub names and hotels, rumours are that he was born here, was married here, died here and there is not a smidgeon of evidence for any of this. And yet, look at the Square with its ravishing apparent historicity and it is irresistible to think he did not saunter by here so that, in fantasy, we could today tap him on the shoulder and ask him if the sonnets are autobiographical. At the time of his life there even lived a family called Shakespeare in the village, but no relationship has been established by even the most determined research. So he must be left in fantasy land while we apply ourselves to other lines of enquiry.

The Square

The Square consists of sixteen houses which used to consitute eighteen homes (nos.20 to 37, some now doubled up) around an oblong tarmacked area. This leads to a pedestrian lane called Duck Lane that runs down to the River Stour and an area of surrounding land of just over three acres that has been used over the years for gardens and allotments. The old privies are extant and the church towers over all, standing on a hump of higher land with the graveyard all around and the medieval rectory next door.

There is a linear plan of the Square included in the chapter 'Properties'.

The Square itself, the oblong tarmacked area, is maintained by Warwickshire County Council but their responsibilities end at the frontage of no.28. Duck Lane is out of their jurisdiction and some of the five houses in front of which it passes own their section, but not all; the ownership of Duck lane could be described as being in stripes. The part of Duck Lane that leads from the houses towards the river appears to be an ancient pathway with no legal owner, as is the land that surrounds the registered gardens, all now defined with fences. The river bank come into this category of unclaimed land. The part of Duck Lane that turns left and leads only to nos.33 and 34 is owned by no.32 and then no.28 and the final small piece by no.33 and its maintenance is best achieved by acquiescence, as is the whole of this interlocking and complicated piece of land.

The Square, before 1905

No.28 is the tall house partly shown on the left, and Duck Lane (first recorded in 1910) leads from the gap beside it. On the right are the three cottages, nos.35,36,37; these are now two houses, no.35 being owned by the Hosking Houses Trust as a writers' retreat. The space to the right of the gable end of no.37 is where the Church House stood. Built before 1656 and demolished in 1885, it had considerable community usage including that of the village school. The corner of the churchyard wall is where the War memorial now stands. St Helen's church had by this date received its renovation and the rectory, built in 1436/7, is behind. The trees appear to be limes.

Photograph lent and restored by Stefan Buczacki

This information was obtained from Warwickshire County Council and is believed to be correct, but has no legal standing.

While the village itself goes back at least to Anglo-Saxon times, the cottages around the Square and down Duck Lane are not as old as they look, being mainly eighteenth and nineteenth century in date. However, there is recent (albeit inconclusive) dendrochronological evidence that parts of no.24 date back to the fifteenth century; certainly it is the oldest structure in the Square and visual assessment places it in the early seventeenth century. If we excavated the Square, underneath the tarmac we would almost certainly find nothing but cobbles and farmyard eco-facts; this is a useful word used by archaeologists to describe the decayed remains of plants and animals, old bits of bone and basket and rotted faeces. There is certainly a lot of this sort of material in the churchyard as the church is certainly pre-Norman in origin and people may have lived here on this convenient hump of land above the flood line of the river from Anglo-Saxon times.

Who knows what Saxon thegn or Norman thug first humped together some tree trunks and plastered them with wattle and daub to make a shelter? And the economic and environmental reasons for choosing this place over one thousand years ago are probably the river, which offered a route through the wooded surroundings as well as easy access to food and water.

The physical presence of the church cannot be ignored; today it still sits like a sphinx above the area and Shakespeare's 'iron-tongued clock' strikes every hour day and night. It contains the oldest surviving stonework in the area and its construction must have strained the resources of the small community a thousand years ago; the reasons why they went to such expensive trouble we discuss later in our chapter on the church. The building today tends to be regarded with nostalgic affection as a setting for life's family events, marriages, baptisms and funerals, and then there are those for whom it remains the house of God, a mysterious and healing place. ◎/◎

Where does history come from?

The past is another country; they do things differently there.
(L.P. Hartley, *The Go-Between*)

Whatever its origins, the village clearly has a long history. But history is notoriously fickle; so how much do we really know about our village, and how much of what we think we know is real?

There are many sorts of history which all have different sources. Historiography is a useful word because it explains the methods people use in the research and writing of history. These are some of them:

Primary sources are the actual, physical data available. This can be archival material (meaning anything written or printed), or buildings and objects, or archaeological data (usually information gathered from excavations).

Secondary sources are one remove from these. They can be documents quoted, a building or object photographed or drawn or some other sort of copy. In these days of the Internet there are lots of opportunities for secondary sources and they are useful because they make material very widely available.

Assumed sources are good guesses or reasonable assumptions, and usually (though not always) informed and educated guesses or assumptions are better than uninformed ones.

Anecdotal sources are based on people's memories and stories; they are not necessarily untrue but they tend to be fallible and can descend into gossip. That is why history can become distorted and sometimes plain wrong.

Primary and secondary sources are what historians rely upon, and the material can be painstaking to assemble and tedious to read, but it is likely to be more accurate than assumed and anecdotal sources which, while fun and interesting, can be misleading.

In this history we make use of all these sources and we differentiate between them, hence this explanation. As an example, this photograph is undated and has no caption, but it is a primary source and there are several copies around in varying condition. It was included in a personal website about the village, which is where we found it, and that is its secondary source. It is assumed that it is of the children at the village school dressed up as knights for their Christmas play of 1965, but the names we have ascribed to the children have depended entirely on anecdotal sources. Just as the history of a conflict tends to be written by the victor, so anecdotal sources tend to be attributed to the person standing nearby holding a pen. Among the quicker ways for neighbours to quarrel is a discussion about anecdotal sources.

Including useful data such as our map reference and height above sea level, there are website entries for Clifford Chambers such as 'British History Online: parishes,' which contain masses of material. But the beauty of the Internet is that it can contain infinite data and no-one need get exhausted because of the ease of skimming and skipping, retrieving pictures and homing in onto details. The personal website we referred to above was and still is being compiled by a village family. It is enchanting to read and will surely in time come to be lauded as an 'authentic voice' (like the writings of St Julian of Norwich). It is anecdotal to its core. It brings material up to the present time and this is important because professional opinion tends to lose interest at some cut-off point, such as the end of the Middle Ages or 1951. This is exactly the point at which anecdotal history takes over, because it is within living memory.

In 1955 the village Women's Institute compiled a 'Clifford Chambers Scrapbook' and also a book about the manor. They are impressive achievements of interesting research and their enthusiasm and range carry through nearly three hundred A4 pages with aplomb. But these twin volumes harbour three problems: one is the lack of any references to sources, so nothing can be checked; secondly entries, even newspaper articles, are infuriatingly undated; and the third problem is one of access. A few photocopied copies circulate but the pictures have become indistinct and it would be ideal material to transfer to the

Internet from the original copy (which is safely deposited in Warwickshire County Record Office) if copyright permission could be granted.

Then in 1965 the Women's Institute of Clifford Chambers entered the National Federation of Women's Institutes Jubilee Scrapbook Competition. With a puce hessian cover, cross-stitched decorated with words and emblems, it is an undated, jumbled mass of interesting bits and pieces.

Both this and the scrapbook by the WI read rather as a woman's view on things. While they are broad-minded and thorough, the river does not even make it into their index (perhaps fishing and boating were then male occupations). We therefore decided, for this book, to

commission a study of the River Stour, because it was probably the reason the Anglo-Saxons settled here in the first place, and also because we know so little about it.

I (SH) asked Stefan Buczacki to write it when I met him at the village postbox at the end of 2012. An experienced writer and broadcaster, he lives in the village and has from the start been a sympathetic supporter of this project. When he kindly enquired how we were progressing, I told him that we didn't know whom to invite to write about the river; that we wanted a zoologist who was also an experienced historian, who would be prompt and brilliant and good-natured. I asked him if he knew such a person and he said 'You know me' so I grabbed him and this is what he wrote.

The school pageant of 'William the Conqueror' 1965
The children's names have been more or less agreed as follows: From left to right, back row (standing):
Nigel Radbourne, Kenneth Jeff, Mavis Giibson, Portia Hopkins, Graham Ullyat, Jane Huckvale, Steve Morris, Dennis Smith.
Front Row, left to right (seated): Philip Wilks, Diana Green, Julian Crang (centre), Kay Betambeau, Peter Grimmer.
Photograph: lent by Linda Pollock

The River Stour

Stefan Buczacki

I grew up and have lived most of my life about as far from the coast in England as is possible. But I have always been very close to a river. In my native Derbyshire I spent my childhood almost literally on the banks of one, so while I have nothing against the sea, serendipity has dictated that I should not join with Helen Cadbury 'in praise of that grey-green merge of water into sky'.

Instead fate decreed I fall in love with rivers, with the wild life on, in and close by them; and with their moods and mysteries. For without doubt, a river is a fickle and strange creature; at once a calm and placid friend on whose banks you can sit and contemplate, lie and dream, make love even or set the world to rights. But on another day in another temper it can turn dark, hasty and threatening, an acquaintance of whom to be chary, an untrustworthy neighbour in a fearful hurry who threatens your home, livelihood, even life itself; in T.S. Elliot's words '...a strong brown god, sullen, untamed and intractable'.

From my beginnings by the rivers Ecclesbourne and Derwent in Derbyshire and brief encounters with the rivers of Hampshire, Oxford's Cherwell and Thames and Stratford's Avon, nearly thirty years ago I appreciatively put down my roots by our Warwickshire Stour. At a mere twenty-six miles in overall length, it is certainly not one of the great rivers of England. Not even its name is unique for it shares it with four other Stours; one in the West Country (flowing through Wiltshire, Somerset, Dorset and Hampshire), one in East Anglia (Cambridgeshire, Suffolk and Essex), one in the West Midlands (Staffordshire and Worcestershire) and one in Kent. The word Stour appears to have several different origins, however, and is not always pronounced in the same way, the East Anglian river name, for example, rhymes with tour rather than hour (as locally) or mower.

Our Stour is almost entirely faithful to Warwickshire, although it rises some three miles across the border in Oxfordshire with a spring near Highways Farm at Wigginton Heath and then enters Warwickshire at Traitors' Ford south-west of Sibford Gower. The river then flows almost due west through the appropriately named village of Stourton before turning north at Mitford Bridge near Burmington where it briefly forms the boundary with Gloucestershire, then along the line of the modern A3400 winding a way through Shipston, Tredington and Halford, Alderminster, Wimpstone, Preston and Atherstone to enter our parish at a point around three hundred yards south-west of Monks' Barn farm which lies some thirty feet above it on the valley side.

The river skirts the eastern boundary of the parish. Indeed for much of its course it actually forms the boundary, only the west bank being ours. Some five hundred yards downstream from Monk's Barn farm, it divides just above a weir to create the leat for the first of the local mills, usually known as the Old Mill. Only one mill is mentioned in our Domesday Book entry and it was probably located here, hence the weir site probably being very old, perhaps Saxon. There was of course no standard spelling then and the village was Clifford at its first mention in 922 and simply Clifort in the Domesday Book in 1086, both meaning the cliff or steep bank by the ford. The ford itself was at the northern parish boundary. Like the residents of Shipston, Atherstone and Preston we could easily have been living in Clifford-on- or upon-Stour, and it is a bit of a mystery why we do not.

The establishment of a settlement here in Saxon times offers no great puzzle, however, because rivers provided not just a source of power for milling but water for drinking and livestock, although wells were important too and several survive in the village. But importantly, rivers and river valleys also provided a ready means of transport. Roads across open countryside, barely more than tracks, were at best impassable in winter and dangerous at all times.

Most of the suffixes in place names relating to rivers seem to have been added in the thirteenth century and it was from then that the demesne land here included not one but two corn mills, although it seems almost certain that both were on the same site; Clifford Mill on Clifford Lane, the B4632, is quite separate and much more recent. Demesne is an old Anglo-Norman term meaning the land possessed by someone and retained for personal use. It appears that the two mills were part of the manor estate that had been given to Gloucester Abbey around 1099 and by 1266 had passed to the office of the abbey chamberlain; essentially the abbey's manager. It was his tenure that added Chambers instead of -on-Stour to the village name, although the first written record of this, as Clifford Chamberere, was not until 1388.

An added reason for believing the weir to be ancient is because at the beginning of the fourteenth century the demesne also included a fishery on the Stour. Little is known about medieval fisheries and certainly nothing about this one, but weirs were often involved; one meaning of the word weir originates with the Old English name for a fence, enclosure or barrier device to trap fish. Intriguingly, its first recorded use in the year 839 relates to a river named Stour: 'Twygen weoras in fluvio qui dicitur Stur' ('two weirs on the river called Stour') but which Stour is not known; perhaps it was ours. The barrier formed by the weir was used to divert fish in to some kind of basket or similar trap. As the traps and the original weir itself were made of wood or other organic material, nothing usually remains, although archaeology on the Clifford weir site could prove interesting. There is no authentic record of a weir fish trap in Warwickshire although there is a possible example at Barford Bridge on the Avon.

The village miller was then a highly important individual in the community; in the thirteenth century our local man was recorded as owning twelve acres and probably served both Clifford and the separate hamlet of Ailstone to the south-east in the neighbouring parish of Atherstone-on-Stour because the tenants of both were responsible for transporting grindstones to the mill. The grindstone worked when water from the mill leat flowed on to the waterwheel itself. At least in its final form, of which part can still be seen, the Clifford Mill had a breast shot wheel whereby the water struck the wheel half way up, which was more efficient than an undershot but slightly less so than an overshot arrangement. The wheel is the only part of the mill machinery that remains and, when working, was fourteen feet in diameter and three feet eight inches wide. There was formerly a second wheel at the opposite end of the building.

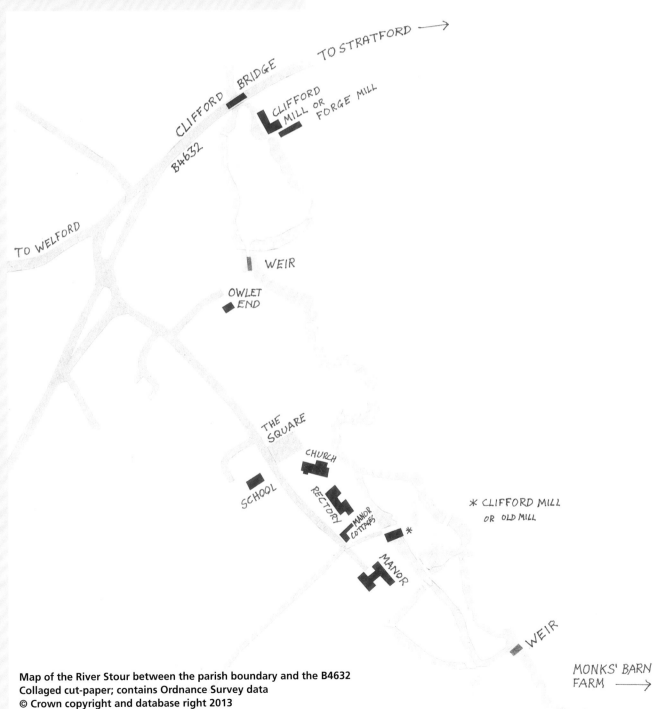

Map of the River Stour between the parish boundary and the B4632
Collaged cut-paper; contains Ordnance Survey data
© Crown copyright and database right 2013

The two mills continued to be leased together with Clifford Manor down the centuries. In the mid-1600s they were referred to jointly as Clifford Mills, but after rebuilding or extending during the eighteenth century they were more usually known simply in the singular as Clifford Mill. The building on the site today is essentially this eighteenth century construction. For no obvious reason, it gradually fell into disuse and it must be assumed that local bakers were obtaining their flour from elsewhere, perhaps more cheaply from Stratford. Certainly by the late nineteenth century all milling had ceased and the building was later used as a laundry for the manor. It seems, however, that the machinery remained essentially in working order because a photograph taken around 1901 shows a handsome wagon outside the mill which was obviously back in business. The miller and baker of the day, Richard Sydney Smith, one of a long-time Clifford milling family who lived at Clifford Lodge, used the old plural name Clifford Mills on the wagon; but that was for a different reason to which I shall return shortly. In 1903 the buildings were sold but seem to have remained a flour mill and bakery at least until the mid-1920s when the site was bought back by the then owner of the manor, Mrs Kathleen Rees-Mogg (formerly Mrs Edward Douty), and an electricity generating turbine for the manor and Manor Cottages was installed in place of the second mill wheel. This was later supplemented by a generator for the church and rectory. From 1933, when mains electricity came to the village, until 1972 the mill was used as farm buildings (a chicken house, piggery, a shelter for turkey plucking) and became increasingly run down. It was then restored as a dwelling and in 1980 a trout farm was constructed on the Danish system. Water from the river flowed through a series of seventeen ponds and back again. For some years the owners reared fine and tasty rainbow trout, but this became uneconomic when the river authority raised the cost of 'renting' the water. The mill buildings then became simply a private house and the ponds were filled in.

To the south of the manor, a right-angled linear pond controlled by a sluice effectively creates an island, while to the north of the manor and just downstream from the mill, the mill leat itself forms a large classical mill pond, deep and mysterious and of the kind much beloved of anglers and poets: one of the ponds Ted Hughes must have had in mind:

It was as deep as England. It held
Pike too immense to stir, so immense and old
That past nightfall I dared not cast.

The main Stour stream passes under a footbridge, sometimes impassable when the river is in flood, carrying a path that is part of the tourist route called Shakespeare's Way before it is rejoined by the mill leat just north of St Helen's church. The courses of the main stream and the leat here form an irregularly shaped island largely occupied by an ancient orchard of gnarled and twisted fruit trees which was once linked to the land behind Manor Cottages and the rectory by another footbridge of which only the abutments remain. From the church the river laps against, and sometimes fills, the gardens at the end of the appropriately named Duck Lane. It was suggested by a former rector, Revd Archibald Pippet, that a ford once crossed the river here but there is no physical or documentary evidence for this.

The river divides again at the weir to the north of the ancient house of Owlet End in the Close, said by some to be the oldest in the village, with the main channel passing through a sluice, then over a weir by the second of the present-day mills, now called Clifford Mill but formerly Forge Mill. It seems to be of eighteenth century origin and at one time was partly in Clifford and partly in Old Stratford, although at this point the boundary now veers westward; so, ironically, Clifford Mill is no longer in our parish. The name Forge Mill dates from its use as an iron forge in the eighteenth century, but it was rebuilt in 1853 as a flour mill and was later acquired by the Smith family who ran it jointly with the Old

The old mill before 1905
Photograph lent and
restored by Stefan Buczacki

Mill, hence the plural Clifford Mills on Richard Smith's wagon. Like the Old Mill, it was bought by Mrs Rees-Mogg in the 1920s, and after the Second World War the renowned Hungarian-born designer Tibor Reich set up his furnishing fabric company there, Tibor Limited. At one time it employed around eighty people, but it closed in 1978, although the splendid brightly coloured woven and printed modernist fabrics can sometimes be bought second-hand. The Shakespeare Birthplace Trust premises in Henley Street have kept his floor to ceiling curtaining in some of the public rooms, where the shadows created by the folds are a component of the subtle pattern of the weave. He died in 1996. We have included him under 'A for Attainment'.

Just above Clifford Mill the two river courses rejoin and leave the parish as they plunge under the bridge on the site of the historic ford. The ford itself had gone by 1266 and the bridge was a subject of much contention over the subsequent centuries, not least because the villagers were responsible for its upkeep. By the seventeenth century it was a three-arched structure known as Clifford Bridge, but because of regular flooding it was rebuilt in 1927 and the road level raised. From here, the Stour passes through Milcote, eventually to end its life to the west of Stratford racecourse where the waters enter the Avon.

Rivers, whether great or small, attract an individual and varied wildlife, and although no great botanical rarities are known from the Stour in Clifford, in one sense this is part of its appeal. That you can pause on its banks and almost know without opening your eyes what plant life surrounds you is in itself reassuring. And when you do open your eyes, you will see those two obligatory waterside trees, the alder and one or more of our native willows, most of them sculpted by the hand of man over the years as the tops have been pollarded. It is remarkable that while a pollarded street tree can look hideous, a pollarded willow on a river bank looks just right. What would many of the great English landscapes be without them? Witness some of those that Constable painted of his East Anglian River Stour. Sadly, our Stour does not have its Constable and I have seen no paintings of the river by the renowned local Edwardian artist William Wells Quatremain who was so fond of the Avon, although he did visit Clifford and painted the manor and the rectory; he is included under 'A for Artistry'.

Other common riverside trees in the parish are ash, oaks, hawthorn, elder, horse chestnut, weeping birch and that woody weed, the sycamore with an understory, quite dense in places like the path at the rear of the Old Mill, of bramble, dog rose, ivy, clematis and sloe among others. At least within the parish the river banks have not been swamped by some uninvited alien like Himalayan balsam as so many other rivers have. We have homely native vegetation, the parasol heads of white umbellifers in assorted variety, stinging nettle, field and creeping buttercups, dandelions, clovers and vetches and carpets of that friendly harbinger of spring unjustifiably maligned by gardeners, the lesser celandine. Within the river, various crowfoots thrive where the water runs shallow and clear, while in the mill pond are brandy bottle water-lilies and clumps of yellow flag grow atop the old weir.

The most obvious animal life too is pretty predictable. Among the mammals, bank vole and wood mouse are common and brown rat occasional, and water vole were once common but are now a significant rarity. I have seen weasels and stoats and there are certainly feral mink. But when did anyone last see an otter in Clifford? Moles and rabbits abound in the water meadows close to the river, foxes are common if usually unseen and there is a large badger sett close by, perhaps one reason why hedgehogs have become scarcer of late. I have regularly seen bats around the river at dusk, and although most are clearly the commonest native bat, the tiny common pipistrelle, there is in fact a treasure trove of unseen richness and rarity at and after sunset because a recent ultrasound survey close to the Old Mill revealed over half our native bat species – both common and soprano pipistrelles with noctule, Leisler's, serotine (just about within its usual range), Natterer's, whiskered, barbastelle, lesser horseshoe (definitely outside its usual range) and the classic water species Daubenton's.

Although I have seen the most water-loving of our native reptiles, the grass snake, in the parish I have yet to see one in the river itself. And to my knowledge, the only local lizard is the slow-worm which must occur nearby, feeding on slugs of which we certainly have plenty. Common frog, toad and at least two species of newt are local and we have abundant invertebrate life including insects from dragonflies and butterflies to midges, as well as molluscs in the shape of slugs and snails. With a river as relatively clean as the Stour, there must be great scope for devoted study; only recently I found freshwater mussel shells deposited on the bank after a flood.

But the great fascination of rivers to a naturalist is that so much remains unseen below the surface; and that, after all, is the ultimate appeal for the angler too, you just never know what will be next to reveal itself. The Stour is a fairly clean river in respect of its water quality, and the plastic bags and other debris deposited after flooding should not mislead anyone into thinking it polluted. There have been odd instances of pollutants in the water in recent times but these are rare and the river fauna itself provides evidence of increasing cleanliness. In the six years from 2000 the number of major groups of invertebrates recorded in the Stour at Clifford nearly doubled from eighteen to thirty-three, and there were increases in the numbers of species found within each group too. The water is consistently alkaline, around pH8 to 8.5, and ranges from a chilling 1 degree centigrade or less in winter to an astonishing 20 degree centigrade, a comfortable swimming temperature (for some!) in summer.

Because of the clean water, we have almost a full quota of the fish species that might reasonably be expected: local anglers regularly take good roach, bream, tench in the slower pools, carp (I have seen fine specimens in the mill pond) perch, dace, gudgeon, barbel and sometimes rudd. Nonetheless personally, and as a traditional angler who appreciates the art of casting to catch anything, I find the modern domination of the coarse fishing pole on the Stour a great sadness. There is now simply no skill in placing your bait precisely where you wish!

The River Stour

Winter floods. The pathway to the old dairy under water

The river is particularly good for chubb, and big pike have been caught, while among smaller species there are minnow, stickleback, ruffe and miller's thumb. I have not seen lampreys, eels or loach, but undoubtedly they occur along with the occasional trout; eels in fact were caught for food by locals in years gone by, as they were in so many English rivers. Of course in times past the river must have been used not only as a source of food but also for transport and then later for recreation too; a few local residents do row occasionally, keeping their boats moored beside their gardens.

It is noticeable, and understandable, that the bird life on the northern side of the village, which comes under the river's influence, differs significantly from that on the south where there is much more of a wood, farmland and hedgerow avifauna. That said, the bird life on and close to the river is pretty remarkable. On the lists of sightings are many species you would expect to have been seen over the years, although most are less common or absent today and include swan, mallard, heron, kingfisher, dabchick, herring and black-headed gulls, cormorant, lesser, greater and cattle egrets, willow and marsh tits, lapwings, corn buntings, skylarks, redwings and fieldfares, finches in variety, goldcrests, coot, moorhen, snipe, jack snipe, redshank, grey and pied wagtails, spotted flycatcher, sedge, reed and marsh warblers, barn, tawny and little owls, kestrel, sparrowhawk and buzzard, crows, pigeons and doves. But there are also many birds you might not expect, like goshawk, hobby and long-eared owl; and lucky were the villagers a few years ago when a young osprey spent a few days fishing here and even a golden eagle paid a visit.

For many residents attention turns to the river only when it exceeds its boundaries; the Stour is no exception, and spills over at least once in most years. 'The river's out' is the local comment when it has flooded the low-lying fields and very occasionally low-lying houses too. But that is what rivers do and that is what water meadows are for. Flood plains are not called flood plains for nothing despite the dreadful consequences for those who live nearby. Some years ago extensive dredging was undertaken to improve the flow, work which incidentally banished our water voles. Efforts continue to be made to minimise damage through the controlled use of sluices and the availability of on-line advance warnings by the Environment Agency, formed in 1996 as the most recent element of the long and complex history of river management which, believe it or not, goes back to the Statute of Sewers passed in 1531 in the reign of Henry VIII to regulate rivers and land drainage. Today, the Environment Agency has the legal responsibility and the legal powers to maintain and improve all 22,000 miles of the main rivers in England. But 'improve' is an emotive word, and in recent years it has become evident that wholesale clearance of water courses and much of the surrounding vegetation – whatever is the riverine equivalent of a scorched earth policy – may be unnecessary. A balance must be struck between minimising flood risk to people and damage to property, ensuring a free flow of water and not ruining the aesthetic of the river and the well-being of its associated wildlife.

Evidence of the astonishing change in the river's moods and effects can be gauged by the range in flow rates recorded at Clifford Bridge over the sample two-year period of 2011 to 2012. At its calmest and most sublime on 2 October 2011 the river flowed at 0.123 cubic metres per second. At its fiercest on 21 November 2012, when some local residents experienced flooding, water was flowing through, and almost over, the bridge at over 400 times this rate: 50.2 cubic metres or over 11,000 gallons per second. Our local automatic recording station for the river level is in Alscot Park where the Stour depth is typically in a range between 0.12 and 0.67 metres. Once it exceeds 0.69 metres warnings of possible flooding are issued. I am sure many residents will recall the time it reached its highest recorded level of 2.86 metres during the great national flood of July 2007. But that was only the highest level since records began in 1958, and undoubtedly in former times it was frequently exceeded. It has become a convention to ascribe all manifestations of the weather that we find inconvenient to climate change, but I am among those who remain sceptical; not about climate change itself but about the fact that it is anything new. It is all part of a fluctuating, if not cyclical, pattern. Floods and other forms of environmental pestilence have been features of our national life for millennia and I have little doubt that in past centuries, when no-one kept records, not only did the Stour regularly inundate the village but skating and perhaps local 'frost fairs' took place on foot-thick ice.

Yes, our River Stour, like all rivers, is a restless and ever-changing influence on the community, as it has been down the centuries. It has shaped the geography and in one way or another much of the social activity of the village and will continue to do so, flowing through this tiny but idyllic corner of Warwickshire long after the residents of today have departed their own modest place in the cycle of parish life. As G.M. Johnson had it: '… when on the scenes of past pleasure we ponder, Fond mem'ry shall hallow the banks of the Stour'. ◎/◎

The upper weir in winter, possibly the site of the medieval weir, then with a fence or basket barrier to trap fish

Local people used to swim in the river; on the major bend opposite Clifford Lodge and on the far side is a short shingle beach, from which the local boys swam in the shallow water. Further out was dark water they believed to be very deep and they never ventured there.   No fatalities are recalled.

No-one is known to swim today because the water is believed (perhaps mistakenly) to be polluted, but either the water really was cleaner forty years ago or people were less fussy.

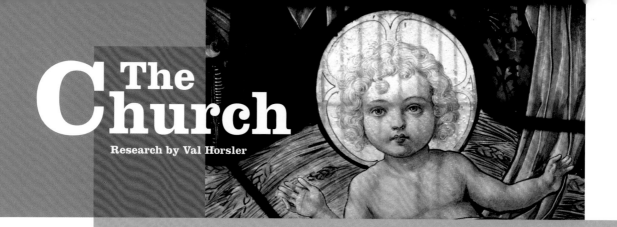

The Church

Research by Val Horsler

Like the river, the church is undoubtedly part of the village's very early history, as the river is probably the reason for settlement here at all. It was an Anglo-Saxon site typically as they liked to settle beside water for their own and animals' usage and the the river would have been their route through the woodland.

In the beginning

We have little idea what form of religious practices took place here before Christianity, so we must rely on educated guesses. The protection of the household and the propitiation of the natural world were certainly paramount, and keeping the river god happy would have been essential; then as now the River Stour floods alarmingly and frequently, but the church, the rectory and the houses in the Square have to this day sat (just) above the flood level; no.28 has flooded in the cellar and no.34 in one room.

We do not have to recall the New World Aztecs to encounter animal and human sacrifice. It is known that the Anglo-Saxons sacrificed animals and possibly humans too, so this may have taken place here on the banks of our familiar river. Blood sacrifice was part of life in the ancient world; the practices of Judaism and of Greek and Roman religion are the most familiar to us, but while we can share closely a classical writer's love of the countryside and springtime, it is foreign to us that they chose to celebrate it with sacrifice.

The Romans are amongst the finest nature poets and their work, when once retrieved by European-wide renaissance scholarship, filtered its way eventually into the Tudor library of Henry Rainsford in Clifford Chambers (see our chapter 'The Poet'). We know Shakespeare read Ovid and Horace, developing their pastoral genre, but the cultural divide is exemplified in one of Horace's odes when, having extolled the beauty of spring, he writes:

Now cut a throat for Fanus in the shadows;
A lamb or kid – whichever he prefers.

The past really is a foreign country: they really did do things differently there. Sacrificing a bull or lamb or goat in what we perceive as a lovely rural setting was their way of celebrating the arrival of the sun again after the 'ice-shelled' winter. We do not know what these people thought or believed or what motivated them above the basic task of survival. When did they dam the river so as to catch fish and build the first of Clifford's two mills? Perhaps the poet Stevie Smith best catches the mood by speaking as the river:

I may be smelly and I may be old
Rough in my pebbles, ready on my pools,
But where my fish float by I bless their swimming
And I like people to bathe in me, especially women.

We know some of what went on from what later became forbidden (if spells are forbidden it means someone is feared to be spinning them) as religion gradually superseded magic. What form of afterlife was entertained is perhaps implied by the Venerable Bede, writing in the eighth century in a monastery in Northumberland. He delved deep and wide into the country's antecedents of belief and, in the brief life of birds, he found a parallel for the condition of men. He described our passage through life as like a sparrow flying through a mead hall on a winter night, from darkness through the light and out again into the unknown dark. However, while Bede used this image to counsel faith in God, it seems that today it is quoted and used for post-Christian secular belief, implying there is nothing in the darkness, only in the light.

Christianity reached Britain under the Romans, but it died out after the legions left in the fifth century, though some emblems of Christianity remained. During the seventh century, the influence of Celtic Christianity and the Irish missionary monks filtered down from the north and the influence of St Augustine and his monks spread from Kent. The Anglo-Saxon nobility were all converted within a century but the original religion remained amongst the rural population until it didn't so much die out as become blended into the folklore of the Catholic Church, here as elsewhere.

Christian monks were peripatetic, walking from place to place and then organising stone crosses to mark the site of their significant orations. Perhaps a wooden or a stone cross was erected on the small mound of land above the River Stour where animal sacrifices had recently been held and so the arrival of Christianity with its message of blood sacrifice, however allegorical, would have been understandable to the people here. Eventually, they would have built a simple church. We can only guess at what it was like; traces of it are said to have been noted in the foundations of the current building and it is likely to have been of wattle-and-daub, and perhaps later of more durable wood, but there is no visible surviving evidence now within the bulk of our stone church.

Nikolaus Pevsner is perhaps the only art historian who has become a proper noun. Over twenty-four years (1951-74) he wrote *The Buildings of England*, criss-crossing the country and making his dry technical analysis of everything of note. Anyone who loves churches will check up in their Pevsner before visiting anywhere, so we quote in full what he says about St. Helen's church.

Both nave doorways are Norman, that on the south side with scallop capitals. There is also a Norman PILLAR PISCINA. In the north side of the church a re-set Early English, low side lancet and a re-set window which is shafted inside. The latter is set in a blocked larger arch of a former transept chapel. The west tower has Perpendicular features, but may be older in its masonry. The chancel is too restored to be valid evidence.

PULPIT Jacobean with blank arches

COMMUNION RAIL Mid or late 17th century

STAINED GLASS fragments

PLATE Chalice with engraved Crucifixion and Paten with Vernicle hallmarked 1494-5

MONUMENTS Two Elizabethan brasses. Sir Henry Rainsford 1622 and his wife, big tablet with two figures facing one another across a bulgy prayer-desk. Two columns; the architrave raised semi-circularly in the middle. Three stiff children in the 'predella'.

The ascetic Professor Pevsner is describing what can be measured and does not so readily entertain those things that cannot. But his incomparable volumes imply that there have been some six major stages in our church's history in which tumultuous events occurred, triggering periods of change lasting some years or even centuries. These were eventually sandwiched between long, uneventful periods when things pottered along.

One of two things usually happened to trigger these surges:

The building altered the way people thought and acted. Changes in thought altered the building. These six surges occurred like tidal waves, and can be identified as:

The great rebuilding (in which a stone church was built, involving and affecting local society)

Introducing Gothic (when it was substantially rebuilt differently)

The Reformation (when religious thought altered)

The Word of the Lord (the translated bible and new liturgy established)

Victorianisation and modernisation (the fabric made strong and comfortable)

Post-Christian secularism (the verdict is still undecided)

The great rebuilding

The parish system developed in the tenth century, possibly founded on an earlier social and land structure. Stone churches were being built, usually as minsters housing communities of monks, nuns and priests, but from just before the Norman Conquest, small parish churches were built, usually by the lords of the manor.

What was probably a wooden structure above the river at Clifford Chambers, perhaps on top of who knows what sacrificial awfulness, was rebuilt by the dominating Normans, some time after 1066. They held the manor after the Conquest and so would have had the economic means to build this, involving everyone around, using manpower and oxen, horses, tools and food having to be found for them all. They would have masterminded the stone rebuilding and the north and south entrance arches survive. The south doorway has its scalloped capitals and worn egg-and-dart pattern, the stone being in alternating yellow and grey limestone, and the north door is plainer. It was not top-of-the-range Norman building, but care was taken and there may have been a carving in the tympanum (the semi-circular space above the door) or they may have never got around to it.

Above it is a 'mass dial' or 'scratch dial', a kind of sundial intended to indicate the time of the celebration of Mass. As with all such extant examples, the gnomon or pointer is missing; it would then have been in the open air as it needs to be in sunlight to cast a shadow. It has long been encased in the porch and so rendered useless.

The nave of the church would have been much like today in its size, no pillars or aisles, with a low arch leading to a small chancel having a semi-circular curved end apse (as at Kilpeck Church in Herefordshire, which is a particularly good example). A stubby tower would have been at the west end. Tall, narrow windows with an internal splay (based on arrow slits) would in all likelihood have had wooden shutters or wickerwork (leading to the diamond criss-cross of lead holding panes of glass four centuries later) for while glass windows were known (wealthy Romans had them), they would not have been installed here yet in this eleventh-century church.

The chancel arch would have been low and decorated with a painting of the Last Judgement; the whole church would have been colourfully painted, and we discuss this below. Certainly cold but sheltered, light would be from tallow candles, reeds dunked in animal fat, which stink as they burn rapidly; they smell like mutton because they are mutton but in time, bees kept could give wax for better candles. The floor was beaten earth at first, probably with rushes in winter and with no seats, the old could lean against the walls (leading to the phrase 'The weakest go to the wall'), the chancel would have had an altar with a cross, the whole edifice representing a huge achievement of local labour and Norman organisation.

The Domesday reference for the village as it then was in 1086 records a church and priest with one plough (which indicates that a carucate of land was attached to it). The record for the village is included with several others belonging to the manor of Tewkesbury: (we give word translations in Italics).

In Cliffort, 7 hides (unit of taxable land) belonging to the same manor [Tewkesbury]. There are 3 ploughs in demesne (land belonging to the lord of the manor) there; and 14 villeins (villagers) with 5 ploughs, and a water-mill worth 12s, and 2 acres of (pasture) meadow. All together there were 13 slaves and female slaves, and a church and a priest with 1 plough. It was worth £8; now £6. The queen gave this land to Roger de Busli, and it paid geld (tax) for 4 hides in Tewkesbury.

There is a story of thwarted love, politics and revenge quoted in the WI History of Clifford, for which we can find no evidence whatever. Aelfgar and his son Beorhtric were powerful Saxon thegns, and Beorhtric became the ambassador of King Edward the Confessor to the court of Flanders at Bruges. Apparently he met Princess Matilda, who fell in love with him; he rejected her advances, and she went on to marry William, Duke of Normandy (who was a rather better catch). After his conquest of England, he avenged the slight to his wife (now the queen) by imprisoning the man who spurned her and giving her all his lands. It is from primary sources we know that Queen Matilda owned the manor briefly and then gave part of these Tewkesbury holdings to Roger de Busli and his wife, who in their turn handed it on to St Peter's Abbey at Gloucester. This medieval arrangement gave rise to the village's name as we describe below.

There is only assumed evidence that the village ever had a monastery. When the manor became the property of St Peter's abbey in Gloucester, it would have been usual for the abbey to maintain a small community of monks living where the manor house now sits, or to send monks to minister to the people. They would have managed and worked the demesne land for the benefit of the abbot at Gloucester. As their calling also required, they would have given what educational and medical care they could to the community and the later dissolution of the monasteries was a major blow to the welfare of everyone both here and everywhere.

Again according to the colourful WI History, when the abbot and his monks were being turned out at the dissolution, the abbot refused to go until he was driven out by fire. He cursed all future inhabitants of the manor, so that no one who lived there would ever be happy. In any event, it is said that when the manor was rebuilt after the 1918 fire, the then owner Mrs Douty placed a bible and some coins in a wall cavity to lay the ghost, if there was one.

In 1891, when the manor had long been remodelled as a domestic house and during the building of a ha-ha in the manor house gardens, about thirty skeletons were uncovered, all male apart from one woman and a child, and all neatly buried on an east–west alignment, apparently in the Christian tradition. They were about four feet below the surface, their heads were laid on stones with other flat stones each side of the skulls to stop them being crushed, and there were no coffins or weapons. Many more skeletons are believed to have remained unexcavated on the site.

The conclusion was that there could be no conclusion. An epidemic would have taken both men and women, violent death would have shown on the bodies, and a monastery would not have included the woman and child. Dating techniques in 1891 were not well developed, so no period for them can be ascertained. Until new excavations are started, it will remain a mystery and the claim for any sort of monastery remains unproven.

Both the edifice and the priests who served it were a development in sophistication; only the manor in the middle ages would have been built in stone. The Saxon people would have lived in wood and wattle huts, probably above the flood line in the Square and where the rectory now stands. They were not free to leave the area; they would have been bound by their labour here and they were an occupied nation.

People were looked after, at least in theory, by the pattern of parishes that was already established by the twelfth century and by the clergy and officers of the church, and they were also controlled. They cared for their own, migrants were not welcome, and for centuries the church and monasteries gave what social care there was. The church would have been their main diversion from a short, hard life of work and procreation, though they would have enjoyed themselves with their community and folk festivals whenever possible.

Groups of parishes in time formed a diocese under a bishop, but he had no control over when and where churches were built or by whom. They were the work of the lords, as here at Clifford Chambers, who regarded the church as their own personal property, along with the advowson, or the right to appoint the priest, and by the beginning of the thirteenth century the system was broadly in place. The list of rectors at St Helen's starts in 1274 and they are French names until the fourteenth century. Services were conducted in the chancel in Latin while the populace stood in the nave.

Life for most was, to quote Thomas Hobbes, 'solitary, poor, nasty, brutish and short'. Belief in the Christian God, by contrast, offered a gentler, more loving message, even if the hope of an afterlife of eternal bliss was tempered by the fear of a hell of dreadful torments. The Christian God, unlike malevolent or capricious pagan deities, was a constant part of daily existence, and His church was there to oversee every part of life from birth to death, its rituals welcoming new babies into the world, seeing them through their adulthood, confirming them in marriage and burying them in the comforting hope of better things thereafter.

There developed saints' days through the remainder of the middle ages, which started as days of remembrance for a particular saint, but became jollies during which another day was taken off work, until the Reformation eventually cancelled them.

We do not know when the church was named after St Helen but we can make a good guess as to why. In Stratford, only two miles away and still accessible today along a clear, direct path-track, there existed from the thirteenth century the Guild of the Holy Cross. It owned the Chapel of the Guild for its ecclesiastical purposes and it was rebuilt in 1424/5. At the very end of the fifteenth century (1496), Hugh Clopton left money for alterations and this probably included the several fresco panels about the mythical life of St Helen who was reputed to have found the true cross.

A head of St Helen from the Folio of the frescoes of the Guild Chapel entitled, 'A Series of Ancient Allegorical Historical and Legendary Paintings', which were discovered in the summer of 1804 on the walls of the Chapel of the Trinity (belonging to the Guild of the Holy Cross) at Stratford-up-Avon, Warwickshire

From drawings made at the time of their discovery by Thomas Fisher FSA Published 1836.

By permission of the Shakespeare Birthplace Trust

We discuss the enigmas surrounding St Helen under our section, 'A for Association'. Sufficient here to say that she was with historical certainty the mother of the Roman Emperor Constantine who, in 311, was suddenly converted to Christianity. He made it the official religion of the remains of the Roman empire which included England, where myth erroneously insists that Helena or St Helen was born. She was credited in legend with having found the true cross in Jerusalem and it is historically accurate that she founded churches on the site of the Nativity and Golgotha. She is therefore associated with Jesus' cross and churches dedicated to her are common.

The veneration of the cross was part of nearby Stratford's religious and economic life and, while we do not know if this depended on a relic of the cross, it is likely to have done so. There are listings of such relics which were probably brought back by crusaders; St Mary's Collegiate Church in Warwick had one and also Holy Trinity in Stratford. It is highly likely that the medieval Guild of the Holy Cross in Stratford would have possessed such a relic, kept at the Guild Chapel. Perhaps they had a small, spare splinter (one medieval splinter looks much like another) and so when Clifford Chambers was revamping its church in the thirteenth century, what could have been more convenient than to send it over the hill in its reliquary and name the church St Helen's?

For there would have been a reliquary with the supposed remains of the true cross so what happened to it in the holocaust of the Reformation? Removed,

burned or buried? It would have been of poor quality by national standards; probably a small casket of oak, covered in gilded tin, with cabochon-cut semi-precious stones such as quartz. It would have been credited with healing powers which, through placebo and for want of anything better, may have had a beneficial effect.

Saxon and Norman buildings were generally based on military architecture, and churches had often doubled up as defensive castles, with arrow-slit windows and thick walls. The Gothic awakening was not only a new form of building, but a new way of thinking and it is as clearly exemplified in our village church as anywhere. Between three and four centuries after they had constructed their Norman church, they somehow summoned the energy, skills and means to rebuild it and the people of the time made several attempts at this over the next eight centuries.

Once Norman architecture fell out of fashion, it won few aficionados until modern times. In the mid-nineteenth century, the small Norman church at nearby Charlecote was viewed with scorn by the new mistress of the manor: 'I had long wished to pull down the wretched old church and build a new one'. She had her way in 1848 when the old building was demolished, 'not one stone was left upon another' and a pupil of Mr Barry's, who designed the new, Victorian Gothic Houses of Parliament, came and designed a new church as it is today. Fortunately, no incumbent of our manor thought to demolish our Norman church, perhaps because it was updated several times in its history. ◎◎

Introducing Gothic

The structural problem with Norman arches was that, being semicircular, the weak point was at the top in the middle. They solved this sometimes by the sheer weight of the supporting masonry, but a weakness it remained. Perhaps it was the overlap of round arches in blank arcading, making a pointed shape, or perhaps it was the strong structural shape of an egg that instigated the pointed arch. This was the ignition for the Gothic revolution and many lecturers have squeezed an egg on its pointed end to demonstrate its strength and, by association, the strength of the pointed arch.

This new structural form altered building, besides art of all sorts, painting and sculpture, clothing and artefacts and eventually printing. It also altered thought in that it sought to admit light, for whereas previous buildings had tried to protect people inside from attackers outside, with gradually improving social safety, windows could expand to admit light and so activity in the church was able to develop as they could now see what they were doing.

Gothic is basically any architecture, and it is usually church architecture, that has pointed arches.

In England, it lasted from about 1180 until 1520 when other ways of doings things intervened. That said, there are different sorts of Gothic and St Helen's has elements of most of them.

Early English Gothic about 1180 – 1250 characterised by simple pointed arches, little tracery and unadorned interiors

Decorated Gothic about 1250 -- 1350 involving complex, sometimes asymmetrical tracery and deep cut ornamentation

Perpendicular Gothic about 1350 – 1520 evolving into sophisticated stonemasonry, using dominant vertical stone shafts to reduce wall structures and increase glass-window size

From the 1530s they were pulling down ecclesiastical buildings rather than putting them up, mainly because of the Reformation but also because of a new interest in building houses. Buildings of the Elizabethan era, from 1563 to the 1600s, is called Elizabethan or domestic Gothic and many churches (including St Helen's) have an Elizabethan window or two, using the pointed arch (just) but concerned to let in the light, not only sunlight into the nave but also the light of understanding.

There are also terms such as transitional Gothic when a window is neither one type of Gothic nor another but a stylistic mixture. Later there is revivalist eighteenth-century Gothic, or neo-Gothic (of which Alscot Park near Stratford is an example). The Oxford Movement or Victorian Gothic determined the rebuilding of the Houses of Parliament as well as St Helen's choir, while pastiche Gothic occurs when the style is centuries out of date but nostalgia asks to carry on the tradition; our war memorial is pastiche Gothic.

The word 'Gothic' is spelt with a capital letter because it is a proper noun and refers to the Goths who were a Germanic people who, one way and another, helped recast the post-Roman world. It was first used as a term of abuse as being everything not classical, but it is now a universal word for a beloved international style.

Once someone has become acquainted with the different sorts of church Gothic architecture, a church can be 'read' and its development be understood. With this information, the stonework of St Helen's silently tells us how our church has evolved.

By about 1180 or 1200, roughly a century after the Norman church had been built, enthusiasm for the new-fangled Gothic arrived. The church was largely rebuilt and was expanded in size on one of the only two occasions in its history, with a transept chapel being added on the north side. There is no evidence but a good guess suggests that this may have been a chantry chapel where prayers were said for the dead; these were usually built and endowed by the lord of the manor. The Reformation decommissioned purgatory and so the chantry chapels were abolished finally in 1547 and the priests dismissed, the chapels pulled down and the treasures dispersed. These priests had offered what education there was to the local community so did this loss lead to the building some time later of the Church house with its small school ? This is discussed in Nat Alcock's chapter on 'the Properties'.

One reason for this surmise is that two miles west, the church at Weston-on-Avon had a chantry chapel, built at much the same date and demolished at much the same time as our chapel.

Whatever was the purpose of this extension, on the inside of the church, on the north side is the remains of a large Early English arch in yellow stone, simple and in its characteristic shape, showing us where this chapel was. Pointed in the same shape as the basinet helmets of the time (armour shapes followed church shapes) this ghost of the chapel is now marked by the four-light window of Tudor Gothic which replaced it and presumably dates from the time of its demolition. Beside the outline of the arch is a small Early English column with base and capital, which may have originally been in another part of the church and was moved here as a form of decoration; it does not seem to have any other function. This typical EE capital with its deep undercutting, roll decoration and simple round pillar is a rural, bastardised, incompetent version of the EE style that was used with such triumphant sophistication elsewhere.

There are two windows at St Helen's whose tracery could, just, count as decorated Gothic with typical curlicue tracery. It was not a style that lasted long, one

Early English lancet window

Decorated window and grotesque

theory being that the stone pieces were complicated to carve and piece together and, when the country's population was decimated by the plague, there were not enough stonemasons left to work the stone.

Perpendicular was much simpler because straight stoneware is easier to carve than curved; the same is true of wood. The wooden door under the Norman entrance arch is probably fifteenth-century perpendicular, as it has the features. The porch which protects it was originally erected in the fifteenth century although the present one is Victorian. According to Nikolaus Pevsner,' the tower has Perpendicular features, though its masonry may be older.' Professor Pevsner sounds a little weary of St Helen's and even its devotees have to acknowledge that it is not one of the most beguiling or interesting midlands churches. Perhaps he dashed us off in a morning knowing that glorious Holy Trinity in Stratford was waiting for him.

There was a small amount of alteration in the early sixteenth century and that really completes the architectural survey of the building until the Reformation. Later stonework repaired the ravages wrought by the Reformation and three centuries later, the Victorian Gothic improvers also arrived but it is not only the stone but the interior appointments that need to be recalled.

Professor Pevsner and indeed all of us would be astounded if we could see what the nation's churches and cathedrals looked like in their prime, before the holocaust of the Reformation. For their interiors were coloured throughout, the windows had coloured glass and the clean stone and white walls that characterise England's 16,000 churches today are foreign to their original concept.

Churches from the eleventh to the thirteenth centuries would have been lime washed throughout in a whitish colour. Then the entire interior would have been painted with red lines all over the interior, pretending to delineate the joins of the building blocks underneath, and at intervals there would have been red rosettes, perhaps set in squares. Gradually, figures of the saints were painted onto the red-delineated walls and there would have been a Last Judgement scene depicted on the Norman chancel arch above its entrance.

Paints were simple, not for them powdered lapis lazuli from Afghanistan, but powdered brick or red earth were used for red, blue was from copper scrapings and lamp-black for black; egg albumen and water were their suspending medium. Twelfth century wall paintings were usually painted onto wet plaster and have consequently lasted well but thirteenth century work was applied to dry plaster, easier to work but less permanent; thus we have far more paintings from the earlier period. These paintings may not have been very sophisticated, here or in any small church, but the connection with Stratford may have meant that better craftsmen were available than a small village could normally muster.

There are no signs at all of these paintings today which may suggest that they were thirteenth-century and so have not lasted. Two miles away at Weston-on-Avon, significant remnants of paintings have recently been found, and they are of the standard, or rather better, that one would expect in a tiny place. It is unfortunate they have completely vanished at Clifford Chambers, and we can speculate whether they showed the life of St Helen.

All the church's windows would once have been filled with coloured glass showing pictures for the illiterate congregation, including Bible stories and almost certainly the life of St Helen. At a time when colour in people's lives was limited to rainbows and the flowers and berries of a much shorter flowering season than today, and when any sort of learning or narrative was limited to what they would find at church, these were persuasive influences. In the vestry at St Helen's, there are fragments from this plenitude of medieval glass that are in their detail interchangeable with similar fragments at Holy Trinity Church in Stratford. These suggest that there was a city depicted in the original window, which might well be from a panel showing St Helen and Jerusalem. These are intriguing issues that would benefit further study and could imply there were connections with the wall paintings and glass at the Chapel of the Holy Cross in Stratford. ◎◎

The Reformation

Both nationally and locally, from the royal palaces to St Helen's, from the great monastic endowments to the thousands of collegiate and local country churches, the Reformation altered thought, conduct and finances as well as the interiors and appointments and government of every ecclesiastical establishment in the land. Some believe that the national imagination has never recovered and that it is due to this that our culture did not produce a colourist until the painter J.M.W Turner, three centuries later.

The Reformation, or the re-formation of the Catholic Church as it then operated, was not one event but a series. Starting with Martin Luther nailing his challenges on the church door in 1511, to the Elizabethan Settlement in 1559, the order and contents of the churches, their governance, the conduct and theology of the clergy besides the nature of worship and expectations of the congregation were all radically altered, then altered back and altered again.

The basic facts of the English Reformation are well known: Henry VIII defied the power of the Pope and declared himself head of the English church. Part political, part financial and part theological, Henry requisitioned the wealth of the church and the monasteries; this process was continued under the rule of his son, Edward IV when Protestant theology became dominant.

St Helen's and most other churches would have had their wall paintings covered in limewash by the officials in front of the dazed people. Eventually, under Elizabeth, painted texts were allowed and St Helen's has these, though dated later. The glass would have been broken by these same officials, the fragments buried

(from where they were retrieved, probably that is how our few fragments survived) and plain glass installed. The figures of saints and the bells, chalices and patens, candlesticks and altercloths, copes and vestments were all taken by the wagon-load. St Helen's would not have been particularly wealthy but it would have been filled with devotional objects, perhaps including their reliquary containing their precious splinter from the cross. Above all, the altar was refashioned from a mystic place, suggesting blood and sacrifice to a plain table for a shared meal of bread and wine.

We have no record of how the people of Clifford Chambers reacted to these profound changes but there is a record of the responses of one village, *The Voices of Morpeth* by Eamon Duffy; he uses the chronicle kept by their priest from 1520 until 1574, and it is a wonderful book. We were probably much the same in the face of so much change but we didn't have a priest who wrote it down.

There was then a brief return to Catholicism with the accession of Mary Tudor and so all the accoutrements and vessels, crucifixes and altar cloths came out of concealment, the rood screen was restored, the candles lit and all things colourful and scented enjoyed a nervous revival. With the accession of Elizabeth, skilful diplomacy was used to introduce the Elizabethan Settlement of 1559, which helped to allay fears of extremism in either direction.

The square-topped windows in St Helen's are late Tudor, showing a concern for the church after the ideological and architectural battering it had received; for all the material destruction of the Reformation, it did offer the opportunity to think instead of the obligation to behave. The new post-Reformation reliance on preaching as the focus of worship put an added emphasis on the pulpit. Sure enough in St Helen's, the Jacobean carved oak pulpit with its sounding board and reading desk is there to allow the word of the Lord to be proclaimed. In the seventeenth century pews were introduced and they reflected the class divisions of the congregation.

A balcony for the musicians was also built at this time, often called the 'singing loft' as the music was supplied by the fiddles, pipes and voices of the local community. The music may not have been good, but it was all there was available until the Victorian reformers replaced the singing loft with a more genteel organ, which could be played by one person, and who was easier to control than a possibly raucous band.

In the mid-seventeenth century, the chancel was transformed by the insertion of the large Rainsford monument into its north wall. This was for the owners of the manor, Henry Rainsford and his wife, Anne, both of whom were connected to Michael Drayton; the significance of this friendship is explained in the next chapter, 'The Poet'. But after that, for some 200 years, the church was left broadly as it was and fell gently into decay. By the end of the nineteenth century it was in a parlous state, dilapidated and damp. The Rainsford monument had caused the north wall of the chancel to bulge severely, and in other places burials close to

the walls, always a favoured position because of the proximity to sanctity, had caused bad settlement.

But while the building may have settled into its austere, white painted and unadorned state, there were passionate debates about the Bible and prayer book. We include a contribution here about the Bible. St Helen's has a copy of the 1599 Breeches Bible (see below) besides the 1799 prayer book that we feature in our section 'A for Alteration'. Neither are used today. ◎◎◎

The word of the Lord

Contributed by Stephen Prickett

Sometimes described as 'the Rock of Ages', or more modestly, as the basic book of our civilization, our Bible ('Biblia' = 'the books') is in fact the product of fierce debate over many centuries. For Jews the word refers strictly to the Hebrew Bible. Not merely does this not, for obvious reasons, contain the New Testament, but the individual books themselves are arranged in a quite different order. This is not so much that Christians (originally, after all, members of a Jewish sect that became universal) re-arranged the contents of the Hebrew Bible to suit their own purposes, as that the arrangements of both the Christian and Hebrew Bibles date from roughly the same period: that of the invention of the 'codex' or bound, paginated book sometime in the first century. Before then the books of the Hebrew Scriptures were on separate scrolls kept in an open case much like modern pigeon-holes, to be selected as required. Questions of 'arrangement' simply did not arise.

The contents of the Christian Bible have been no less passionately disputed. The apocryphal books, including Bel and the Dragon, Ecclesiasticus, Judith, the two books of Maccabees and Tobit, were included in the Greek 'Septuagint', the Greek translation of the Hebrew scriptures made probably between the third and second century BC. These were then imposed on the Christian Bible for largely political reasons at the Council of Nicea in 325, almost 300 years after the events of the New Testament. Subsequently treated with grave suspicion by Jerome, and other Church Fathers, and expunged by the Protestant reformers (who relegated them to a separate section) they were nevertheless retained in the Vulgate by the Counter-Reformation Council of Trent in the sixteenth century.

But not merely are the contents of our Bible the product of millennia of controversy, so are the translations themselves. The Bible is essentially a translated book. Even the Hebrew Bible uses words from Babylonian, Egyptian, and Ugaritic, with parts of it even in Aramaic, the language of the Persian Empire. The Greek of the New Testament is not the language of the Classics, but Koinē Greek , the common Alexandrian dialect of the eastern Mediterranean traders. But even the Koinē incorporates translations of classical Greek, Hebrew and Latin. Moreover, by the time we reach the English Bible, we must add on the old Latin translation, later superseded by Jerome's Vulgate, and a succession of partial and whole English translations from Wycliffe and Tyndale, to the Calvinistic Geneva Bible, even before the (never-'authorized') 1611 King James version.

Tyndale had been populist; the King James translation, magisterial. Each had its own purpose, its own axe to grind. As a result, unlike other sacred texts, there is no available original text to the Bible, no neutral version from where to start. The huge variety of modern translations is, in short, only a continuation of the polemical pluralism that has always been integral to the history of the Bible from its very earliest origins.

Check list of features and furnishings

In 2003 the Stratford branch of NADFAS (The National Association of Decorative and Fine Arts Societies) was commissioned by Holy Trinity (the mother church) to survey and report on the furniture and fittings of St Helen's. It was completed in 2006 and, in the manner of such reports, it is exhaustively thorough; even the fire extinguishers are listed besides the last little folding card table and sheet of music. But its thoroughness is an asset, as it finds items that might otherwise go unnoticed. Here are six that are most interesting.

The Geneva Bible is often called the Breeches Bible because Adam and Eve made themselves breeches out of vine leaves. This is the version of the bible Shakespeare used. This copy is dated 1599 and is fully bound in gold embossed brown leather. It appears to have been forgotten amongst other books of sermons and family bibles hymnals and prayer books which might be the best way to keep it safe.

The piscina in the south wall of the chancel, up by the altar, is probably the only piece of the Saxon church remaining. A piscina is a shallow basin used for washing vessels used in preparing the sacrament and their use dates back to the ninth century. Ours is a pilaster piscina built into the wall; it is five sided with a small drainage hole, so that water associated with the blessed bread and wine could not be drunk or used by animals but would return to the earth. It is a holy drain.

The font may also be Saxon but is usually believed to be medieval, and even Professor Pevsner steered clear of this anomaly. Heptagonal on the outside, a circular bowl inside and carved from granite and at some point lined with lead, the flat surfaces would probably have had shallow sculptures on each surface that may have been hacked off during Reformation. It may have served for baptism for a thousand years and certainly for over seven hundred years.

The pulpit is essentially Jacobean, the five sided carved 'drum' being of that date, with blind tracery and foliage carved in oak. It has nineteenth-century repairs and candleholders. When King James I commissioned the new translation of the Bible, completed in 1611, it was distributed to all churches and they were expected to read it and teach from it, so a new pulpit would (here as elsewhere) have been a sensible installation.

The pulpit (detail)

The Church

The Bishop's chair (detail)

Graffiti drawing of a deer

The Bishop's chair is in the sanctuary, waiting for a bishop to grace it. This is one of the Rev Pippet's commissions (1911) and was made by J.W. Pyment of the Campden Guild in Chipping Campden. The point of interest is that Chipping Campden was a hotbed of the Arts and Crafts Movement in the early twentieth century, and the Pyments were associated. This splendid seat looks of its time and design persuasion and suggests Revd Pippet's acumen in such matters.

The Superscreen in wood and engraved glass separates the tower from the nave. This is the only instance in the church of any modern design of any quality, and it is lovely. It commemorates James Robertson Black, who was churchwarden for thirty-five years, the sandblasted and cut lettering is graceful and professional. It was designed by David Woulfe who still lives locally, and was installed in 1959.

There are other items of interest such as the clock and the bier, the charity boards and the sedilia, the corbels and the altar rails, the processional cross and the kneelers; this is besides what was probably the leper window, for the distribution of arms to people whom today we believe did not have leprosy but just eczema, psoriasis or some other skin disease. Even this is not an exhaustive listing, only a cherry-picking from the many furnishings but there is one piece of unofficial art, or rather, there used to be. Revd Pippet included this photograph of a scratched picture of what is probably a roe deer, marked as being beside the south door in the church. It has clearly been covered up or obliterated since 1905, but it is included here for its graffiti charm and because it is impossible to date; it could have been roughly carved in the stone doorway at any time from the Anglo-Saxons to the Victorians.

St Helen's was not the only place of worship in the village. From the eighteenth century, there were some non-conformists in the village (often known as 'them methodies') as in most of the villages around and there was a simple chapel on the Campden Road that was rebuilt as a solid art deco building in 1930s . It closed as a chapel during the Second World War and was sold as a private house in 1952 with the proviso that there were to be no wild parties. There was no catholic provision in the village.

Monuments

The eighteenth and nineteenth century monuments inside are legible (unlike many in the churchyard) and pertain to those of a higher class and desire for posthumous reputation than most of our Square residents could expect. The Annesleys who gave the church two generations of rector, and the Nash and the Pippet families have plaques to their memory, but we shall only include here the Rainsford Monument, because it pertains to Michael Drayton, to whom we dedicate the next chapter.

As is usual in churches, the most interesting monuments across several generations are those of the family at the manor who held the power to appoint the church's priests during the time of the church's building or repair.

In St Helen's, the oldest monuments within the church are the series of Rainsford family brasses from the sixteenth century, which now hang on the north wall of the chancel. Those of Hercules Rainsford and his wife and children were originally inserted into the top of an altar tomb in the north-east corner of the nave. Until the 1886 restoration the pulpit sat partly on top of this tomb, obscuring the children apart from their heads. The tomb was in the way of the changes planned in 1886 and was also in a bad condition, so it was taken down and the brasses re-erected on a slab and hung on the wall. Hercules, who died in 1583 aged 39, is shown bare-headed and in armour next to his wife Elizabeth and above their three children, two sons and a daughter. Another brass depicts this daughter, Elizabeth, and her baby.

The brasses reveal a poignant family history. Hercules died young and intestate. His wife Elizabeth obtained letters of administration over his affairs the day after he died and married William Barnes six months later. Of Hercules and Elizabeth's three children, the elder son, also Hercules, died young and the daughter Elizabeth, who was baptised on 1st October 1581, was only twenty when she died in October 1601, presumably in childbirth; she had married Edward Marrowe. Her baby daughter, Frances, did not survive her long and was buried on 7 January 1602.

Of the three children on the first brass, therefore, only one, Henry, survived to rear his own children and he too had to endure the death of one of his three sons. Henry Rainsford's memorial is the large, striking monument in the chancel. Born in 1575 and so aged only eight at his father's death, Henry was Hercules Rainsford's sole heir and was made the ward of his stepfather, William Barnes, who appears to have cared for him well. According to earlier records there was once a monument in the church to William Barnes too, noting that he lived with Elizabeth for thirty-six years and died in 1622 aged seventy-six.

Henry was knighted in 1603 and married Anne Goodere; their friendship and patronage of Michael Drayton is celebrated in the chapter 'The Poet'. They had three sons, one of whom, William, died young and is portrayed on the monument in his swaddling clothes alongside his brothers. Above his head are the words 'Of such is the Kingdom of God'.

As with the tombstones in the churchyard, there have been no large or flamboyant memorials during the last sixty or so years inside the church. This can be regarded as a lost opportunity for commissioning interesting work, as memorials at nearby Preston church to the West family testify. ◎◎

The bells

The bell of the church clock was the time-keeper for the area and the peal of bells was used for expressions of local or national joy and danger; in the Second World War it was an agreed signal of invasion that all church bells throughout the country would be rung.

St Helen's would have had bells before this set of eighteenth-century replacements, but it was the accelerating Industrial Revolution that made these enduring new castings available.

St Helen's has a ring of six bells, four of which were cast by Matthew Bagley in 1771, the fifth also by Bagley in 1773 after his original casting failed, and the sixth, a new treble bell, in 1946, by John Taylor of Loughborough at a cost of £500.

The frame and fittings for the original five bells in St Helen's were made by Barwell of Birmingham in 1904, with new ball bearings fitted by Taylors in 1946, when all the bells were retuned and the new treble added in a separate frame. St Helen's bells are inscribed as follows:

1 MB MADE ME THE LEADER OF THIS PEALE TO BE 1771

2 M BAGLEY MADE ME 1771 JOHN SMITH WILLIAM COOKS CHURCH WARDENS

3 MB MADE MEE 1771 JOHN SMITH WILLIAM COOKS CW

4 JOHN SMITH WILLIAM COOKS CHURCH WARDENS WILLIAM [???] BAGLEY MADE ME 1771

5 AND NOW I HOP TO PLEASE YOU ALL AND SING TO THE GREAT CREATERS PRAYS MY FATE HATH BEEN UNFORTUNATE BE FOAR MY SELF COULD RAIS MATTHEW BAGLEY MADE MEE 1773

The inscription on bell 5 appears to commemorate the earlier failure of casting. The new treble bell of 1946 is called the Peace Bell and is dedicated to the villagers who gave their lives in the Second World War; its inscriptions read as follows:

DEDICATED TO THE FALLEN OF CLIFFORD CHAMBERS 1939–1945 KENNETH ENGLISH, FREDERICK PINFOLD, JOHN SALMON, DOUGLAS MOLE

and on the other side

PEACE 1945 PEACE I LEAVE WITH YOU. MY PEACE I GIVE UNTO YOU.

The bells used to be regularly rung by the village team, but are rarely rung today, though teams sometimes visit. Charmian Evans (who lived at no.30) joined the team in 1977 and remembers the advice given her by Kath Radbourne (who lived at no.34) when she started: 'Always breathe in when you raise your arms; otherwise, your bra will ping up and you'll be left with no support for the rest of the session.' Kath Radbourne was a bell-ringer for over sixty years and when she died in 1988, they rang a muffled peal in her honour.

The bell-ringing team, about 1905

The church before its renovation in 1886 showing the smaller chancel. Pippet could not have taken this photograph as it predates his appointment, but it is included in his archive.

Victorianisation and modernisation

'The chancel is too restored to be valid evidence'

So said Pevsner and he was one of those who realised how destructive the Victorian restorers had been. They appreciated the Gothic form, but only when it was cleaned up and with its palimpsests of meaning scraped away. In the same manner as the restoration of the cottages in the Square, too much was done and the old thrown out and replaced with clumsy imitations, but such interference does stop the building (whether cottage or church) falling down.

In 1886, therefore, a major restoration was carried out at St Helen's at a cost of £1,500. This involved not just repair and restoration of severely compromised medieval fabric but considerable alteration as Sir John Maclean said in his article on the church in Transactions of the *Bristol and Gloucestershire Archaeological Society* (vol 14. 1890): 'The result was a determination to carry out a thorough restoration of the sacred edifice, and we have all learnt by this time what that means. Architects are not content with simple restoration, they must make some improvements of their own, and generally destroy some of the most interesting and characteristic features of the ancient structure committed to their charge.'

The main changes were to the chancel, which was rebuilt and extended to the east. A new pitched roof was added, and internally stone carved heads of the twelve Apostles were installed in a frieze along the north and south walls. The narrow Norman chancel arch was pulled down, widened and rebuilt higher, demolishing the area that would have had the medieval wall painting of a Last Judgement (as at Stratford's Guild Chapel). Much of the north wall of the chancel was demolished to make way for an organ chamber

with a vestry behind it, reached through a new door in front of the altar rails. It was now that the small window in the north chancel wall was removed and repositioned in the vestry, and old stained glass found in the tops of the nave and chancel windows was incorporated into the new vestry window.

In the nave, among other minor changes to the layout, the table tomb of Sir Hercules Rainsford with its monumental brasses was found to be in a dilapidated state and was removed, and the pulpit, which had previously partly rested on this tomb, was moved into the north-east corner of the nave. Outside, gravestones displaced by the extension of the chancel were set up against its eastern wall. These practical repairs were essential, but there were other influences that determined our present church. ◎◎

The Oxford Movement

In the 1830s, a group of able and influential people in Oxford sought to question what was by then nearly three centuries of austere Protestantism in the Anglican church, regarding its theology, conduct and church appointments. While the ins and outs of the politics of this group need not concern us, it did affect churches throughout the land by bringing colour back into them. This involved new stained glass and painted interiors, vestments and accoutrements, the use of incense, lighted altar candles, revised liturgies, ancient hymns reintroduced, processions, dressed altars, vestments, genuflections, making the sign of the cross. While adherents to this new attitude also went and ministered to the people during outbreaks of cholera and made service to the poor, they had an effect in St Helen's that we can see today. This includes the array of modest vestments and altar items, the east end stained glass window and furniture such as the bishop's chair, and the effect of brass, candles, glitter and the smoke of holiness.

Since that major refurbishment there have been further changes, some decorative and others designed for comfort and ease of use. The east window was reglazed in 1899 with a new stained glass design showing scenes from the life of Christ; illustrated in our section 'A for Anger'. The church clock on the tower was bought and installed in 1901; that there was an earlier clock is clear from the churchwardens' accounts of 1792, which record the payment on 1 April of 14s 6d to John Rogers for winding it. Electric lighting arrived in 1930 and heating was installed the following year. In 1932 the choir stalls were renewed, the altar lengthened and the sanctuary retiled; more recently, the vestry has been extended. Now we have a red Wilton carpet and activating mechanism for the entrance door, but where is the congregation and the priest? ◎◎

The rectors

The modern parish of Clifford Chambers extends over some 1,725 acres, with a large proportion of its fifteen-mile boundary running along the old county border between Warwickshire and Gloucestershire. Its northern boundary with Stratford was fixed in AD 970 in a charter issued by Oswald, Bishop of Worcester, but there have been changes down the centuries; in 1928, for example, parts of the parish of Weston-on-Avon were subsumed. And notably, in 1931, the parish was moved administratively from Gloucestershire to Warwickshire when the county boundaries were rationalised, although for ecclesiastical purposes it remained part of the diocese of Gloucester until May 2001 when it was transferred to the diocese of Coventry. St Helen's is now part of a greater parish with Holy Trinity church, Stratford.

The living at Clifford was once one of the most valuable in the diocese, and its rectors as a consequence were people of major significance in the hierarchy of the church. Many of them also held major posts elsewhere and neither lived in Clifford nor visited it. Edmund Frowcester, for example, who was rector from 1501 to 1529, was also the Dean of Hereford Cathedral. The 'cure of souls' and the day-to-day church work were carried out by curates.

Sir John Maclean researched and published a list of rectors in 1889/90, but there were gaps which were filled in the early 1900s through the work of the Revd Hockworthy, who also found the previously elusive names of some of the curates. Although both ecclesiastical and secular records give bits and pieces of information about St Helen's rectors down the centuries, it is clear that in most cases they were titular office holders only, and would have had little to do with the church and its parishioners. A full list of rectors and a partial list of curates were published by Nat Alcock in his architectural survey and history of the rectory.

The survey established that the rectory always stood on its present site, in a position convenient to the church, and a dendrochronological analysis of six timbers from the roof all gave the date of felling: the winter of 1433/4. Building certainly therefore commenced during 1434, when one John Bokeland was rector. He had assumed the post in 1414 and held the office for several decades, resigning it by 1458. Very little is known about Bokeland beyond the fact that he became a member of the Stratford Guild of the Holy Cross the year after he was appointed at Clifford.

His decision to build a house in Clifford, and his association with Stratford, make him unusual. Might he be the link with the Chapel of the Holy Cross in Stratford, and did he instigate the naming of our church after St Helen? ◎◎

'Riotous assembly'

In 1529 after the resignation of Edmund Frowcester, as Nat Alcock reveals in his history of the rectory, Arthur Cole was given the Clifford living by the Archbishop of York, but a few weeks later Arthur Chadwick ousted him, claiming that the next presentation had been granted by St Peter's Abbey, Gloucester, in 1517 to one John Docwra, who had in due course presented Chadwick. Given that the advowson belonged to St Peter's, Chadwick's claim would appear to have been a strong one; but Cole had sued for reinstatement, claiming that his appointment had been made in proper form by Cardinal Wolsey with the approval of the Bishop of Worcester. Chadwick took his case to the Star Chamber, and his plea describes a dramatic occurrence at the rectory:

'One Arthur Coole, clerk, pretendyng an unjust title to the same, ryotously asembled with Robert Johnes, clerk, John Turner, husbandman and Richard Cotton, cardemaker, came unto the benefice with other ryotous persons to the number of 12, whose names to your seyd orator are unknown, with longe bowes and hande gonnes, and they brake oppon lockes & doores of the same benefice & parsonage ryotously & contrary to your pease, and there by myght expulsed and put out your seyd orator and hys fermor from hys seyd benefice ... [requests] that the seyd reyotous persones may be so punyshed that theyr punyshment may be to the most feyrfull example to all other such lyke offenders.'

The Star Chamber had jurisdiction over such acts of 'riotous assembly'. Cole's response was that Chadwick had obtained possession in Cole's absence and that later Chadwick had left and Cole had taken possession 'without any resistence yn peasyble maner', and he was therefore not guilty of any riot. Despite the strength of Chadwick's claim, Cole appears to have kept the benefice; in reality, he was probably a more influential figure than his opponent, and his willingness to resort to violence was simply too intimidating. Cole's later history does indeed indicate that he was a person of considerable weight. He held other livings in Yorkshire, Gloucestershire and Berkshire, was a canon of St George's Chapel, Windsor, was in Cardinal Wolsey's entourage and appeared to have maintained his position even under Queen Mary. Most of Cole's career was spent at Magdalen College, Oxford, where he ended up as President before dying in 1558. He took little further interest in Clifford, where he was recorded as non-resident in 1551, and he left nothing to the parish in his will. Presumably, however, he benefited considerably from his rectorship's rich endowments.

As time went by, some at least of the rectors appear to have had local connections and to have been resident in the rectory. Details of these and of the curates who ministered to the people of Clifford are included on our website, but here we we discuss the best known of the Clifford rectors, Revd Pippet.

Archibald Pippet served as rector from 1895 until 1918. Initially he lodged at the New Inn and then at Stratford while building Red Hill, his own house in the village, so that he need not leave Clifford when he retired.

Apart from his twenty-three years ministry, he gave the village several enduring gifts. One is the collection of glass negatives of the photographs he took here and nearby, now in the Warwickshire County Record Office. They are enchanting but they are special because they are of a place that has outwardly changed so little. They date from 1895 to 1906 and they were presented to the village in 1980 by his grand-daughter.

The commissioning of the church's east end-window of stained glass is discussed under our section 'A for Anger' and the war memorial under 'Agony and adoration'. Both are fine commissions by designers who were the top of their professions, but Revd Pippet's acumen and taste in such matters does not end there. We also mention the Bishop's chair in the sanctuary, made by the Campden Guild, as was the stained glass in the lancet window in the north wall, and he apparently designed the brass ewer and bowl used at baptisms, besides commissioning the church clock. Records show he needed the usual faculties for these installations and while we know he paid for the main window, did he subsidise the rest?

The parish magazine for 1930 describes him as follows.

'William Archibald Pippet was an outstanding teetotaller, and in this was a great example for the temperance cause, but he was not at all bigoted in the matter and, like St Paul, would allow wine for the stomach's sake. Neither was he narrow minded with regard to other forms of worship as the laying of a stone by him at the building of the Chapel in Campden Road testifies.
Of the great work at the school accomplished by Mr Pippet as chairman of the school managers and official correspondent for the school it is almost impossible to estimate.....it has been acknowledged very freely that it is one of the best schools in Gloucestershire for the training of the young...one evidence being that all the young men of the parish who returned from the war went straight back to work. No dole for them!
The influence of such a character of upstanding rectitude among us has had for good cannot be estimated and put into words.'

Both the Revd Pippet and his wife were buried in the churchyard in 1930. ◎◎

Portrait of him from the Pippet archive

Post-Christian secularism

The church today is, like many village churches, a shadow of its former self. In the 1950s, the Stratford Blue Bus used to bring people from town because the owner of the bus company so enjoyed Canon Brookes' sermons. In the parish magazine of 1954 there was on Sunday, Holy Communion at 8.30am, also Matins at 11.0 am once a month, Children's service 2.30pm and Evensong at 6.30pm. At St Mary's at nearby Atherstone (also under Canon Brookes) there was an Evensong every Sunday at 3.0pm and Holy Communion once a month. That church is now a private house.

Today, there is one service each Sunday at St Helen's led by a lay reader or priest from Holy Trinity. As an objective take on the matter of dwindling church attendance, we have included here some attendance figures for these plus Sunday plate takings for a complete year.

For the calendar year from June 2012 until June 2013, there were 963 attendances at services. This does not include children who only attended in any numbers at one baptism (7), Easter (4), Harvest (12), Remembrance Day when poppies are laid on the steps of the War Memorial (21) and Christingle Service (34).

The average or mean measurement of adults attending was 18.5 per service. The mode was 12 (the figure that occurs most frequently)

With an electoral role of 404 (excluding children) these attendance figures speak for themselves.

Plate takings for the same year were £5,640 and this represents the main part, albeit not the total, of St Helen's income. It costs a minimum of £13,000 per year to pay the diocese fee and run the church and, while St Helen's has some capital resources, its revenue income is inadequate.

We have considered in some detail the reasons why people do and do not attend church services under our section 'A for Attendance', and also the future for churches that their community no longer wish to support under 'A for Apathy'.

Perhaps modern scepticism is best expressed by Philip Larkin in his poem 'Church Going', written in 1954. Nevertheless, his dying words in 1985 were, "I am going to the inevitable".

'Church Going'
Philip Larkin

Once I am sure there's nothing going on
I step inside, letting the door thud shut.
Another church: matting, seats, and stone,
And little books; sprawlings of flowers, cut
For Sunday, brownish now; some brass and stuff
Up at the holy end; the small, neat organ;
And a tense, musty, unignorable silence,
Brewed God knows how long. Hatless, I take off
My cycle-clips in awkward reverence,

Move forward, run my hand around the font.
From where I stand, the roof looks almost new-
Cleaned, or restored? Someone would know: I don't.
Mounting the lectern, I peruse a few
Hectoring large-scale verses, and pronounce
'Here endeth' much more loudly than I'd meant.
The echoes snigger briefly. Back at the door
I sign the book, donate an Irish sixpence,
Reflect the place was not worth stopping for.

Yet stop I did: in fact I often do,
And always end much at a loss like this,
Wondering what to look for; wondering, too
When churches fall completely out of use
What shall we turn them into, if we shall keep
A few cathedrals chronically on show,
Their parchment, plate and pyx in locked cases,
And let the rest rent-free to rain and sheep.
Shall we avoid them as unlucky places?

Or, after dark, will dubious women come
To make their children touch a particular stone;
Pick simples for a cancer; or on some
Advised night see walking a dead one?
Power of some sort or other will go on
In games, in riddles, seemingly at random;
But superstition, like belief, must die,
And what remains when disbelief has gone?
Grass, weedy pavement, brambles, buttress, sky.

A shape less recognisable each week,
A purpose more obscure. I wonder who
Will be the last, the very last, to seek
This place for what it was; one of the crew
That tap and jot and know what rood-lofts were?
Some ruin-bibber, randy for antique,
Or Christmas-addict, counting on a whiff
Of gown-and-bands and organ-pipes and myrrh?
Or will he be my representative,

Bored, uninformed, knowing the ghostly silt
Dispersed, yet tending to this cross of ground
Through suburb scrub because it held unspilt
So long and equally what since is found
Only in separation   marriage, and birth,
And death, and thoughts of these – for which was built
This special shell? For, though I've no idea
What this accoutred frowsty barn is worth,
It pleases me to stand in silence here;

A serious house on serious earth it is,
In whose blent air all our compulsions meet,
Are recognised, and robed as destinies.
And that much never can be obsolete,
Since someone will forever be surprising
A hunger in himself to be more serious,
And gravitating with it to this ground,
Which, once he heard, was proper to grow wise in,
If only that so many dead lie round.
◎◎

Chancel east end window in St Helen's church by T.F. Curtis Wood and Hughes, dedicated 1899, showing the Virgin and child

War Memorial in the Square by Ninian Comper, dedicated 1919, showing St George and the dragon

Roger Pringle is the former Director of the Shakespeare Birthplace Trust and an authority on Elizabethan verse and culture. In 2010, the Hosking Houses Trust invited him to present a talk about Michael Drayton, a Tudor poet closely associated with the village, in the church of St Helen. He has contributed this chapter at our request.

'The Muses Quiet Port': Clifford Chambers and Michael Drayton

Roger Pringle

In the course of its quiet, rustic history Clifford Chambers has not been the birth or dwelling place of a Prime Minister, an Admiral of the Fleet, a famous inventor or any other national celebrity. But it can boast the distinction of being associated with one of the writers who contributed significantly to creating, during the reigns of Queen Elizabeth I and King James I, a golden age of literature: Michael Drayton. Though the level of acclaim which Drayton's work attracted in his lifetime was not sustained in later centuries, his place in the list of the most notable English poets is secure. The leading literary figure of his age was, of course, William Shakespeare. They were both Warwickshire-born, near contemporaries, and followed similar careers. Later, I shall consider the likely relationship between them and the part that Drayton's association with Clifford may have played in it. Meantime, my focus is on looking at how Drayton's connections with the village came to be forged, and to show how his affection for it and the surrounding countryside found expression in his work.

Drayton's links with Clifford were the result of the circumstances of his early life. He was born in 1563, a year before Shakespeare, in Hartshill, a village near Nuneaton in the north of the county. His social background was similar to Shakespeare's: farmers, butchers and tanners figure in the sixteenth-century family records. Information about his childhood and schooling comes from the writer himself. From passages in his poetry and various prefaces it is clear that his boyhood was spent partly in the household of Sir Henry Goodere, whose family seat, Polesworth, was near Hartshill. In 1597, dedicating one of his historical poems to Sir Henry's nephew, Drayton referred to 'the happy & generous family of the Gooderes (to which I confess my self to be beholding to, for the most part of my education)'. In another dedication he paid tribute to

'that learned and accomplished Gentleman, Sir Henry Goodere, whose patience (was) pleased to bear with the imperfections of my heedless and unstayed youth. That excellent and matchless gentleman, was the first cherisher of my Muse'.

Sir Henry, a prominent figure in the county and beyond, was a man of literary interests and counted the poet Sir Philip Sidney among his friends. It was the young and impressionable Drayton's good fortune to spend time under his roof at Polesworth. In verse written towards the end of his life, the poet recalled his early ambitions to be a poet:

In my small self I greatly marvelled then,
Amongst all other, what strange kind of men
These poets were; and pleased with the name,
To my mild tutor merrily I came,
(For I was then a proper goodly page,
Much like a pigmy, scarce ten years of age)
Clasping my slender arms about his thigh.
O my dear master! cannot you (quoth I)
Make me a poet, do it; if you can,
And you shall see, I'll quickly be a man...'

We do not know who Drayton's tutor was or where he received his schooling, though the likelihood is that the tutor was engaged at Polesworth itself. Other references in the poet's writings recall the influence of the Gooderes on his upbringing and choice of future career. Dedicating a collection of odes, in 1619, to Sir Henry Goodere's nephew, who succeeded to his uncle's estates, Drayton recalled the times when they gathered round the fire at Polesworth to be entertained by a minstrel:

These lyric pieces, short, and few,
Most worthy Sir, I send to you,
To read them, be not weary:
They may become John Hewes his lyre,
Which oft at Polesworth by the fire
Hath made us gravely merry.

Drayton's role within the Goodere household may have extended to becoming a tutor himself to Sir Henry's two daughters, Frances and Anne. Frances, the elder, who was probably about six years younger than Drayton, was the dedicatee of his verse epistle about Lady Jane Grey, published in 1597, two years after her father's death. In his dedication the poet spoke of 'the love and duty I bare to your father whilst he lived' and recorded with pleasure: 'My self having been a witness of your excellent education, and mild disposition (as I may say) ever from your cradle, dedicate this Epistle of this virtuous and goodly Lady to your self…' But it was to Sir Henry's younger daughter, Anne, that Drayton apparently formed a deep attachment, which probably began when he assisted with her girlhood education at Polesworth and matured over his lifetime. It was the bond that would link him indissolubly with Clifford Chambers.

Anne was born in Coventry, presumably in the Gooderes' town house, in 1570/1, making her about eight years younger than Drayton. Her childhood and teenage years were spent in the country at Polesworth. Whatever intensity of feeling the poet held for her seems to have been transmuted in his verse into an idealised love relationship. She became his muse, inspiring poems in two of his earliest volumes, 'Idea, the Shepheards Garland', 1593, and 'Ideas Mirrour', 1594, the first being a series of pastoral poems influenced by Edmund Spenser's 'The Shepherd's Calendar', and the second comprising fifty-one sonnets. Drawing on the Platonic notion of types of perfection and beauty, compared to which all other persons or things are but shadows, Drayton's Idea stands for his lady and the pure love he holds for her. Although she is not identified by name in these collections, it is clear from topographical references that Anne Goodere is their principal inspiration. The thirteenth sonnet of 'Ideas Mirrour', for example, speaks of the shepherd's wandering years, a fanciful allusion to the poet's youth, spent by the banks of the Anker, the river that ran close to Polesworth. Written in the pastoral and ornamental style fashionable in the 1590s, the sonnet ends with a claim that the countryside and river associated with the poet's Idea can compare favourably with the scenic glories of classical Greece such as Tempe, the beautiful valley in Thessaly, and Helicon, the mountain famous for its springs and sacred to the Muses:

Clear Anker, on whose silver-sanded shore,
My soul-shrined Saint, my fair Idea lies,

…

Lo, here thy shepherd spent his wandering years;
And in these shades, dear nymph, he oft hath been,
And here to thee he sacrificed his tears:
Fair Arden, thou my Tempe art alone,
And thou, sweet Anker, art my Helicon.

Another of these early sonnets, addressed to the River Anker, concludes:

Arden's sweet Anker, let thy glory be,
That fair Idea only lives by thee.

A reader today unfamiliar with this kind of poetic artifice might question the authenticity of feeling being expressed. Using the pastoral genre, though, allowed the poet to avoid being too direct and confessional – or embarrassing – about his affections. After all, it was not for a tanner's son to aspire to winning the love of the daughter of a knight, who in some respects was his boss and guardian. Perhaps it was this knowledge that helps to account for the note of dismay sometimes sounded in Drayton's verses about love. Despite this, however, and the mannered style he often adopted, there remains the impression of a serious, even intense, commitment on the poet's part to his Idea, linked specifically to Anne Goodere, and to a love that could not be returned on any level other than companionship.

Less than a year after the publication of 'Ideas Mirrour', Sir Henry Goodere died; the poet had been a witness to his will, which was proved in May 1595. Among its bequests was the provision of a handsome sum of £1500 to his daughter Anne for her 'preferment in marriage advancement'. Doubtless this event was already anticipated since she married soon afterwards, leaving Polesworth to spend the rest of her life at Clifford Chambers with her husband, Henry Rainsford. A few years her junior, Rainsford had inherited its manor in 1583 when he was only eight, on the death of his father; he was later to be knighted, in 1603, at the time of King James I's coronation. From their marriage in 1595 until his death in 1622, they appear to have been a devoted couple. 'Toujours Loyall' was the family motto inscribed on their impressive commemorative monument in Clifford's church. Fashioned from alabaster and marble, it depicts them kneeling and facing each other, hands closed in prayer, across a prayer-desk. Figures representing their three children, all sons, are in attendance below, one of them, who died in infancy, in swaddling clothes. (see page 40)

The monument is made of painted alabaster. Sir Henry, in armour, kneels in prayer opposite Lady Anne who wears her widow's dress. Between them is a small table with two books lying on a cushion, and under the canopy is Sir Henry's shield with its stag's head crest and his motto 'Tous Jours Loyall'. Their children are below, the surviving sons, Henry and Francis, in armour. Apparently, Lady Anne is not buried here and it is not known when or where she died but she appears to have outlived both her husband and her friend.

The 1886 reconstruction of the church was partly necessitated by the bulging of the chancel wall caused by the erection of the Rainsford monument, and the monument in its turn was badly damaged by water leaking through the chancel's flat roof. In 1967 it was restored, details were reconstructed and cleaning brought to light traces of colour which allowed educated conjecture about the original. The restorer repainted it and replaced the gold leaf; but the original form of Lady Anne's headdress could not be reliably guessed at, so she now has a simple plug on her head.

Piety was one of the virtues picked out in the best surviving description of Anne's character. This comes from an authoritative source, her own doctor, none other than the renowned Stratford-upon-Avon physician, John Hall, Shakespeare's son-in-law. His is a revealing testimony about the woman who had captured the young Drayton's heart, who became and

The Rainsford Monument in the church's chancel

remained his great friend and muse and who was the reason for his association with Clifford Chambers.

It may be a truism to say that history was written by those who could write; but it is a fact that universal literacy is a phenomenon of the last 150 years or so, and before that the lives of the vast, uneducated majority are in many ways a closed book to us simply because they were not recorded. Even among the wealthier and educated classes, writing was for higher things than the trivia of daily life.

But some fragments emerge. Among educated professionals, doctors sometimes took notes about their

patients' ailments and the cures they prescribed. One such physician was Susannah Shakespeare's husband John Hall, through whose records we know something more about the Rainsfords and Michael Drayton. He treated Anne Rainsford in her old age and widowhood for 'the stone', and took the opportunity to discourse on her personal qualities and achievements, describing her as modest, pious, friendly, devoted to sacred literature, and expert in French and Italian. Around twenty years earlier he had cured her husband Henry of a malign fever and associated ailments, including 'hypochondriac melancholy'. The physician also treated the Rainsfords' children and grandchildren, and on one occasion was summoned to Clifford to attend to 'Mr Drayton poet laureate' for his 'labouring of a Tertian', a fever or ague. An emetic infusion was prescribed, intended to make the patient sick, followed by a soothing dose of syrup of violets; the medicine, as Hall observed, 'wrought very well both upwards and downwards'.

John Hall's treatment of Michael Drayton for a fever, from James Cooke's translation of Hall's Latin notes, published in Select Observations on English Bodies, 1657

John Hall's admiring pen sketch of Anne also points to the cultured ambience that would have prevailed at Clifford Manor. Like many sons of the gentry, Henry Rainsford had completed his formal education by being admitted to one of London's Inns of Court, where performances of plays, music and other revels were often part of the social life accompanying the teaching of law. In 1594 he entered Middle Temple, where a few years later Shakespeare's *Twelfth Night* was performed. In addition to overseeing a considerable estate, Sir Henry developed business interests away from his locality, becoming in 1618 a member of the Council of the Virginia Company, active in American colonisation and exploration. On the home front, he was frequently involved in Stratford affairs, held in respect by the town council and included some of its leading citizens among his friends.

One book surviving from Sir Henry's library, bearing his ownership inscription on the title page, gives an indication of the breadth of his reading. It is the first English translation of one of the masterpieces of Spanish Renaissance literature, Jorge de Montemayor's *Diana Enamorada*. Its stories of lovers pursuing one another in disguise and being victims of mistaken identities were a major influence on pastoral writing in several European countries, including England where, in its Spanish original, Diana was a model for Philip Sidney's *Arcadia*. It is known that the English translation was circulating in manuscript some years before it was published, in 1598, and it appears that Shakespeare had access to it, since the romance is an acknowledged source for *The Two Gentlemen of Verona* and echoes of it can be found in others among his romantic comedies.

Continuing references in his poems and evidence from other sources show that Drayton's admiration for Anne was in no way diminished after she moved to Clifford Chambers on her marriage in 1595. Indeed, they make clear that he became a frequent visitor to her home and formed a strong friendship with her husband. In the course of his epic historical poem 'The Barons Warres', published in 1603, the poet recalled his 'virgin unpolluted' verse of some years before and said that if he had not turned to describing the bloody times of England's past,

My lays had still been to Idea's bower,
Of my dear Anker, or her loved Stour.

The geographical shift of his beloved's relocation to the Stour, the river flowing by Clifford, was signalled again three years later in an eclogue which imagines her as a shepherdess:

Driving her flocks up to the fruitful Meene,
Which daily looks upon the lovely Stour,
Near to that vale, which of all vales is Queen,
Lastly, forsaking of her former bower:
And of all places holdeth Cotswold dear,
Which now is proud, because she lives it near.

Drayton anchors his pastoral vision of Anne Rainsford as a shepherdess in the real countryside around her home. She is envisaged tending her sheep on Meon Hill, a prominent feature of the landscape four miles south of her village. From its slopes the Vale of Evesham can be seen to the south-west, while a mile or two further south the land rises to the Cotswold escarpment. Brought up in the more insipid landscape of north Warwickshire, the poet responded enthusiastically to the scenic attractiveness of Clifford's environs, which he was now experiencing on visits to its manor house.

Arriving at Clifford on foot or horseback, Drayton would have made his way down its one main track, passing husbandmen's cottages, barns, a few yeomen's farms and the early medieval church, with its adjacent timber-framed rectory, before reaching the Rainsfords' manor house at the end of the village. Tall, roomy, with its walls featuring closely spaced beams probably sawn from local oaks, the building dominated the village. On his walks the poet would have noted Clifford's working mills by the Stour, the nearby fishery and the orchards and gardens attached to many of the houses. The open fields beyond consisted mainly of strips sown

with wheat and barley, or areas of pasture set aside for sheep grazing. For Drayton, a countryman at heart whose work necessitated spending much of his time in London, and who remained a bachelor, visiting Clifford and being with the Rainsfords seems to have become a regular and valued part of his life. Village and family provided a retreat for renewal of friendships and spirits, and escape from the pressures of life in the capital and from what he described as 'the loathsome airs of smoky cittied towns'. The phrase comes from a section praising Warwickshire in his vast poem 'Poly-Olbion', begun around the mid-1590s and published in part in 1612.

'Poly-Olbion' was described on its title page as: 'A chorographicall Description of all the Tracts, Rivers, Mountaines, Forests, and other Parts of this renowned Isle of Great Britaine'. Derived from the Greek meaning 'many blessings', the title was also a pun on Albion and the decorative title page depicted an enthroned Britannia holding symbols of power and plenty. The work comprises a descriptive section, or 'Song' as Drayton termed it, for every county in England and Wales (an intended coverage of Scotland never materialised), written in lines of fourteen-syllable rhyming verse and averaging about 400 lines per Song. The poem runs to about 15,000 lines as it takes its reader on a journey through the land, celebrating not only natural beauties but legends, folk traditions, historical events and persons on the way.

The poem is one great song of praise and triumph reflecting and contributing to the developing sense of national identity and confidence that characterised the Elizabethan and early Jacobean age. A major influence on the work was William Camden's monumental history, *Britannia*, though Drayton undertook much research of his own and persuaded John Selden, the antiquarian, to provide scholarly notes on the text. He also commissioned maps to accompany each county Song, intended as 'lively delineating to thee, every Mountain, Forest, River and Valley'. Towns and villages are largely omitted unless they relate to some significant legend or historical happening. Thus key elements of the Warwickshire map are scenic features, the fertile Vale of the Red Horse in the south-east of the county being represented by a well-endowed allegorical figure of bounty, and the Forest of Arden affirmed by the presence of a lady of even ampler proportions, with bow and arrows – Diana, goddess of the hunt.

The Song devoted to Drayton's native county, the thirteenth in the sequence, incorporates passages evoking the sights and sounds of the forest, including the dawn chorus in spring:

Then from her burnished gate the goodly glittering east
Guilds every lofty top, which late the humorous night
Bespangled had with pearl, to please the morning's sight:
On which the mirthful choirs, with their clear open throats,
Unto the joyful morn so strain their warbling notes,
That hills and valleys ring, and even the echoing air
Seems all composed of sounds, about them everywhere.

The poet identifies individually the birds which are contributing to the dawn chorus, giving fascinating information on names then in use: for example woosell (blackbird), nope (bullfinch), tydie (goldcrest) and hecco (green woodpecker). After a vivid description of hunting in the forest, an account of a hermit living there and the herbs to be found in the wood, the rivers of Warwickshire are accorded their place in the overall picture:

How Arden of her rills and riverets doth dispose;
By Alcester how Alne to Arrow easily flows;
And mildly being mixed, to Avon hold their way:
And likewise toward the north, how lively-tripping Rea,
T'attend the lustier Tame, is from her fountain sent:
So little Cole and Blyth go on with him to Trent.
His Tamworth at the last, he in his way doth win:
There playing him awhile, till Anker should come in.

The entry of Anker in the list diverts Drayton into an extensive digression on its association with Anne Goodere, specifically named, before resuming with the story of the Avon and concluding:

Scarce ended they their song, but Avon's winding stream,
By Warwick, entertains the high-complexioned Leam:
And as she thence along to Stratford on doth strain,
Receiveth little Heil the next into her train:
Then taketh in the Stour, the brook, of all the rest
Which that most goodly Vale of the Red-horse loveth best.

The final flourish of the roll call of rivers ending with the Stour can be taken as yet another compliment to the lady who once dwelt by the Anker. And Coventry too was hymned in the Warwickshire Song as having had the good fortune to be the birthplace of one Anne Goodere.

It may well be that some of Drayton's work on this daunting project proceeded while he was staying with the Rainsfords at Clifford. But, since the village at this period was in Gloucestershire, one has to turn to that county's Song, the fourteenth, for a revealing mention of it:

...dear Clifford's seat (the place of health and sport) Which many a time hath been the Muses quiet Port.

This Clifford reference occurs in an extensive passage during which the Vale of Evesham is made to wax lyrically about itself, claiming that vales in general exceed the attractiveness of hills, though Meon is singled out as a model of what a hill should be:

Clad in a gown of grass, so soft and wondrous warm,
As him the summer's heat, nor winter's cold can harm.

The Song leads from the Vale to the Cotswolds, taking interest and delight in sights that doubtless struck Drayton on his walks in the area. The Cotswolds had long been famous for its breed of sheep, whose wool had become one of the key export commodities of medieval England, and upon whose wealth the sun-coloured limestone churches, tithe barns, manor houses, and cottages of the region were built. The poet enjoyed capturing the characteristics of its sheep and the merrymaking of the shepherds; the fanciful map illustrating this Song depicts a shepherd on top of Meon hill, while further south a group of shepherds in the vicinity of Chipping Campden are dancing round a flagpole with a banner inscribed 'Heigh for Cotswold'.

Although this may relate to a typical sheep-shearing feast or similar revelry, it may possibly be a reference to the Cotswold Olympic Games, an annual event believed to have started in 1612 as the brainchild of Robert Dover, a lawyer who had recently moved into the area. As his Olympic Games developed in the second and third decades of the seventeenth century its fame spread far beyond the locality. That Drayton witnessed the games and knew Dover well is certain, for one of his later pastoral poems is entitled 'To my Noble Friend Mr Robert Dover on his brave annual Assemblies upon Cotswold'. This poem, published in 1636 after the poet's death as part of an anthology celebrating the games, praises Dover for reviving the 'Golden Age's Glories', enumerates some of the Grecian sports and predicts that country people living in the Cotswolds and the Vale of Evesham will keep alive the memory of his games in song and story. It seems certain that his intimate knowledge of the games, taking place not far from Clifford, derived from the times he stayed with the Rainsfords.

The fact that these visits also brought him into the vicinity of Stratford raises the question as to whether he and Shakespeare were friends. It is usually taken for granted that they knew each other, and it is sometimes claimed they were close friends, mainly on the basis of an entry in the diary of John Ward, Vicar of Stratford, dating from the early 1660s: 'Shakespeare, Drayton and Ben Jonson had a merry meeting, and it seems drank too hard, for Shakespeare died of a fever there contracted'. This was recorded about forty-five years after Shakespeare's death, and thirty after Drayton's, but there were people still alive in the town who could remember the dramatist, including his daughter Judith who died in 1662. On the face of it the anecdote is credible, though given Drayton's reputation among some of his contemporaries for temperance and sober living it seems out of character to hear of him going on a bender. There must, however, be a strong presumption that if the 'merry meeting' did indeed take place it was while Drayton was staying with the Rainsfords.

There are good reasons for supposing that Drayton's path must have crossed with Shakespeare's during his visits to Clifford. As mentioned, Henry Rainsford was a well-known figure in the town, and some of his friends there knew Drayton and were close to Shakespeare. One of these was Thomas Greene, who had met and become close to Rainsford when they were both at the Middle Temple and share with him a taste for literature. Greene also became acquainted in London with Drayton, composing a sonnet in praise of the poet in 1603 and in another poem, written in the same year, making glancing reference to two poets he judged to be among the most honourable of the time: Samuel Daniel and Drayton.

In 1603 too Greene moved to Stratford, having been appointed its town clerk, a role he filled for the next fifteen years. Shortly after coming to Stratford, he was also appointed as steward on Rainsford's Clifford Chambers estate, and by 1609 is known to have become a tenant of William Shakespeare's at New Place, the spacious house close to the town centre purchased by the dramatist in 1597 and his home until his death. In a memorandum dated 9 September 1609, Greene noted that he 'might stay another year at new place'; in fact he appears not to have moved out until 1611. Greene refers three times in his diary to Shakespeare as his cousin (though this may not perhaps imply a relationship in the strictly modern sense). He was subsequently involved in consultations with Shakespeare in response to plans to enclose land which affected their interests, before eventually leaving Stratford in 1617. Given Greene's admiration for Drayton, and his close connections with Shakespeare and Rainsford, it is not difficult to surmise that they all gathered occasionally for a 'merry meeting' when Drayton was on one of his visits to Clifford Chambers.

Henry Rainsford shared another mutual friend with Shakespeare: John Combe, member of a leading Stratford family and one of the wealthiest men in town. When Combe died in 1614, Rainsford acted as an overseer of his will, and he, his wife Anne and Shakespeare were all recipients of monetary bequests.

Other links existed between the Rainsfords, the Shakespeare family and by association Drayton, for example the fact that John Hall, Shakespeare's son-in-law, was the Rainsfords' family doctor. The doctor was also on familiar terms with Thomas Greene, treating his daughter and acting with him in 1613 as joint trustees in a property settlement.

This network of Stratford-Clifford friendships and connections reinforces the likelihood that Drayton and Shakespeare met from time to time, in the town or the village. It is also likely they encountered each other in London where Drayton lived for most of his adult life, and where from 1598 until 1604 he too was involved in its theatre world. He collaborated on about twenty plays for the Lord Admiral's company, one of the two leading acting troupes in the capital, the other being the Lord Chamberlain's for whom Shakespeare wrote and acted from 1594 onwards.

Yet though we can be confident they knew each other, there are grounds for concluding their friendship was not close. First, Drayton seldom missed an opportunity to acknowledge important friends and patrons by dedicating to them books of verse or individual poems, or by making complimentary references within his poetry. There is no such dedication to Shakespeare. Moreover, if they had been intimates one would expect some tribute on Shakespeare's death or as a contribution, of the kind Ben Jonson made, to the prefatory poems written for the publication of the dramatist's First Folio. Even more telling is that Drayton's one and only reference to Shakespeare seems somewhat short on admiration or affection. In his two-hundred-line 'Epistle to Henry Reynolds', in which he paid tribute to many of the leading writers of his time,

The Poet

Drayton allocated Shakespeare a mere two couplets:

Shakespeare thou hadst as smooth a comic vain,
Fitting the sock and in thy natural brain,
As strong conception, and as clear a rage,
As any one that trafficked with the stage.

This is undoubtedly somewhat pedestrian and lukewarm in its praise, especially when compared with the more approving recognition given to others in the poem, which describes how Drayton and his friend, the poet and critic Henry Reynolds, would gather round a log fire in winter, with food and drink, to share their love of literature.

What the poet felt he owed to his host, by contrast, was sounded in a long elegy he composed following Rainsford's death in 1622, titled 'Upon the Death of His Incomparable Friend, Sir Henry Raynsford Of Clifford'. Though the poem engages in some sorrowful breast-beating and supposed frustration at not finding words to articulate his grief, it expresses with much feeling the sense of a friendship deeply missed. Sir Henry was a person 'past all degrees that was so deare to me', who has shown 'his care of me where ever I have been'. In his life he proved:

A man of so much vertue, knowledge, wit,
Of natural goodness, supernatural grace
...
A spirit so brave, so active, and so free
...
Besides so liberal of his faculties,
That where he would his industry bestow,
He would have done, ere one could think to do.

Drayton concludes by lamenting the death of 'one who was a thousand friends'. Apart from the inscription on his monument in Clifford church, this is the only detailed description we have of the devoted husband of Anne, the poet's muse, and stands in relation to him as John Hall's memorable words do to her.

Sir Henry was succeeded at the manor by his son, also Henry, though Anne evidently continued to live there, possibly until her death though it is not known when and where she died, nor where she is buried. A letter from her son to his uncle from Clifford, dated 1632, bears a postscript saying 'My mother remembers her very kindly to your self and Lady'. It is also clear that Sir Henry's death did not disrupt Drayton's pattern of visiting the family or that his poetry had continued to keep alive his lifelong identification of Anne as his standard of perfection in matters concerning womanhood and a muse both to inspire and to be imagined in his poetry. In 1619 he published a poem called 'A Hymne to His Ladies Birth-place' which, as previously in 'Poly-Olbion', developed more elaborately the conceit of dismissing Lady Godiva as the traditional reason for Coventry's renown in favour of it being the place where his Idea came into the world, even pinpointing the street where she was born, Much Park Street, which still survives near the cathedral. He suggests that her birthplace should become a famous shrine, and that the well-known incident of Godiva's ride through the streets was but a preparation for the coming of one more honourable, whose house should be the site of annual birthday celebrations:

Of thy streets, which thou hold'st best,
And most frequent of the rest,
Happy Much Park every year,
On the fourth of August there,
Let thy maids from Flora's bowers,
With their choice and daintiest flowers
Deck thee up, and from their store,
With brave garlands crown that door.

Drayton clearly intended the tongue-in-cheek elements of humour in the poem to appeal to Anne, and perhaps expected her to glimpse many years of heartfelt admiration behind the playfulness.

We shall never fully understand the poet's relationship with his Warwickshire lady friend. As noted, his personal poetry tended to be framed in Platonic terms, which viewed love aroused by beauty leading to spiritual enlightenment and satisfaction. It does not follow that because Drayton treated of matters of the heart on a philosophical plane he was not himself a man of passion. Nevertheless, if autobiographical significance is to be found in his poetry, and to some extent he invites this, it is not the physical side of human relationships that is sounded. Whether linked to Anne, or to other women in his life, or concerning lovers in history and legend, his love poetry steers away from the explicitly sexual. William Drummond, the Scottish poet and critic, touched on his friend Drayton's cast of mind when discussing contemporary poets who had written memorably about love. He singled out Sidney, Daniel, Spenser and Drayton, but qualified his praise of the latter because 'he seemeth rather to have loved his Muse than his Mistress; I know not what artificial similes this showed well his mind, but not the passion'.

Some of Drayton's finest love poetry, however, breaks free from decorative and stylised language, laced with hyperbole and classical allusion. He was capable of achieving a subtle and lively expression in which thought and feeling were brilliantly fused, as in his sonnet beginning:

An evil spirit, your beauty haunts me still,
Wherewith, alas, I have been long possessed...

And he could produce another sonnet which competed with Shakespeare at his best, though it is entirely Drayton's voice that is heard, blending true emotion with elements of self-mockery:

Since there's no help, come let us kiss and part,
Nay, I have done; you get no more of me,
And I am glad, yea glad with all my heart,
That thus so cleanly, I myself can free,
Shake hands for ever, cancel all our vows;
And when we meet at any time again,
Be it not seen in either of our brows,
That we one jot of former love retain.
Now at the last gasp of love's latest breath,
When, his pulse failing, passion speechless lies,
When faith is kneeling by his bed of death,
And innocence is closing up his eyes,
Now, if thou would'st, when all have given him over,
From death to life, thou might'st him yet recover.

Who inspired these love poems, if indeed it was any single person, is not known. They may or may not have

44

been largely autobiographical. Whatever paths his love life took, it seems certain that it never embraced marriage. His portraits suggest someone of a pensive, if not melancholy inclination. The best one depicts him in fashionable gentleman's clothes, his head crowned with a laurel wreath, symbol of the poet, though his blue-grey eyes look at us sadly, with no hint of a smile to offset the stern demeanour. This impression is reflected in contemporary opinions about him. In 1598 Francis Meres commented that Drayton was regarded by all sorts of people as 'a man of virtuous disposition, honest conversation, and well governed carriage'. Six years later, in an anonymous play performed by Cambridge students, he was said to lack 'the one true note of a poet of our times, and that is this, he cannot swagger it well in a tavern, nor domineer in a hothouse'. Some years after his death, Thomas Fuller described him as 'a pious poet… very temperate in his life, slow of speech and inoffensive in company.'

Recent analysis has confirmed that the painting of the laurel leaves is contemporary with the portrait, and the date 1599 corresponds with Drayton's age at the time. After the death of Edmund Spenser, he was a contender for the laurel wreath of poetry but it was not an official appointment until 1670. The laurel leaves had been associated with poetry since earlier times, and are here as an acquired attribute, rather than representing an appointment.

Portrait of Michael Drayton by an unknown artist
Oil on panel, 1599 © National Portrait Gallery

45

Dedicating himself at an early age to the poet's vocation, he appears to have lived austerely in pursuit of his ideals. He was a perfectionist, constantly revising and improving his work; sometimes poems consisting of hundreds of lines were substantially rewritten. He counted eminent people amongst his friends, received praise from his literary peers and was widely published and read in his time. Yet he seems to have struggled to make a living, leaving an estate at his death worth only a little over £24, partly, it would appear, because he was not sufficiently adept at working the patronage system on which writers depended. There are signs of personal insecurity in the sensitivity he showed about his artistic and social status. His wish to be portrayed wearing a laurel wreath was a way of laying claim to a laureateship role before the position had been formally instituted; and on the strength of being one of the attendants or esquires accompanying Sir Walter Aston, a major Warwickshire estate holder, at his investiture as a Knight of the Bath in 1603, Drayton paraded the title 'Esquire' after his name for the rest of his life.

Though Drayton attracted a wide circle of friends, backers and admirers from London, Warwickshire and elsewhere, it is fair to claim that his relationship with Anne Rainsford was a key one in his life, and that after her marriage the manor house at Clifford provided him with what he may well have regarded as a second home. A late twentieth-century critical study (Jean R Brink: *Michael Drayton Revisited*, Boston 1990) has attempted to play down the importance of Drayton's involvement during his formative years with Sir Henry Goodere and his family, and challenged the significance claimed for his relationship with Anne, partly on the basis of suggesting that the poet had reasons later in life for exaggerating his accounts of his upbringing. It may be true that Drayton had grounds for embroidering his Goodere connections; he may have romanticised his attachment to Anne (many poets' muses owe something to fictive treatment); he may have had in mind other women when writing some of his love poems; he certainly enjoyed the support of friends and patrons, of both sexes, besides the Gooderes. None of this, however, undermines the case for concluding that there existed an exceptional and enduring bond between him and Anne. Since no letters, diaries or other personal documentation survive relating directly to them, the compelling evidence for their special relationship rests primarily on the references to her, her husband and to Clifford Chambers and its countryside, found in verse written over a thirty-year span. 'I am more than a fortnight's friend', wrote Drayton; 'where I love, I love for years; which I hope you shall find'. Though these words were addressed to a literary soulmate, the Scottish poet William Drummond, they could have been vouched for by his Lady Anne.

The evidence, disclosed in his poetry, of his valued relationship with her is underpinned by the certain knowledge that he was a regular visitor to Clifford Manor, probably from the time of her marriage to Henry in 1595 until his death thirty-six years later. Between 1618 and 1631, when he died, Drayton corresponded with William Drummond. In the handful of their letters that survive three of Drayton's, years apart, refer to absence from his London home due to being in the country. In April 1619 he mentioned his recent return to the capital from the country 'where I have been all this winter'. Two years later, in November 1621, he explained to Drummond that his failure to keep in touch was partly due to 'my long being in the country this summer'. Ten years later, months before his death, he informed Drummond that the letter he was writing would be delivered by a mutual friend whom he had met by chance 'at a knight's house in Gloucestershire, to which place I yearly use to come, in the summer time, to recreate my self, and to spend some two or three months in the country'. This letter is dated 'Clifford, in Gloucestershire, 14 July 1631, in haste'. It is entirely plausible to assume that the two earlier instances of his being away in the country related partly or wholly to visiting the Rainsfords, and that they all connect to a much longer pattern of staying in the village. Nor is it fanciful to imagine that Drayton's wish to 'recreate' himself involved using the long periods away from London for creative work. His

late poem 'Nimphidia, the Court of Fayrie', published in 1627, a mock-heroic evocation of fairyland owing not a little to *A Midsummer Night's Dream*, may bear signs of being composed at Clifford, and not just in its general awareness of country people's folklore traditions and beliefs. At one point Drayton localises the story of his diminutive fairy world by having Pigwiggen, the lover of Queen Mab, suggest that the best place for a secret assignation '…is that fair cowslip flower, On Hidcote hill that groweth'. The reference, dropping so unexpectedly and delightfully from Drayton's pen, is to a hill about five miles south of Clifford. Its mention is the only topographical reference of its kind in Drayton's seven-hundred-line poem, yet diminutive as it is, like the cowslip and the fairies who look to make love there, it tellingly signifies how Clifford and its environs became interfused with the landscape of his imagination and how he was never far from remembering the family home there to which he resorted on many occasions.

In his elegy in memory of Sir Henry, the poet made mention of his faith:

But that I am a Christian, and am taught
By him who with his precious blood me bought,
Meekly like him my crosses to endure.

He would have accompanied his hosts to their village church, St Helen's, on Sundays, along with many other communicants from the rural community. Whereas the old manor house no longer exists, mostly destroyed by fire in 1918, the church still stands. Though considerably changed since Drayton and the Rainsfords worshipped there, many features from their time survive, including the font where Anne's children were baptised. Doubtless, the trials and tribulations that undoubtedly beset Drayton, glanced at in his elegy above, were more easily managed not only through prayer but also by sharing them with his two incomparable friends in Clifford. It was their home which served him, year in and year out, as a loving milieu and temporary refuge from the storms of life, or, as he described it, 'the Muses quiet port'. ◎◎

Full text with references and further illustrations are on www.hoskinghouses.co.uk under *Round the Square and Up the Tower*: 'The Poet' by Dr Roger Pringle

Map of the Warwickshire rivers, showing the Stour with a mermaid at the bottom, from 'Poly Olbion', the thirteenth song

Published 1613
By Permission of the Shakespeare Birthplace Trust

A History According to 'A'

We have selected twenty-five words beginning with 'A' and matched them with pictures to illustrate aspects of parish life. We have avoided cute pictures of toddlers, family pets and girls on horses which, however charming, did not contribute to issues we think interesting. We also made two exceptions to our rule whereby we only include photographs of people who no longer live here and these are under 'Affection' and 'Appetite'.

1 Abnormality

These photographs show three of the exterior grotesques which decorate St Helen's, but which have no purpose except ornamentation and perhaps the concealing of a join between stones. They are probably early or mid fifteenth-century, possibly reworked and certainly repaired. We have featured elsewhere some of the church's gargoyles, which are usually carved to carry a waterspout from the guttering and to project the water away from the walls.

In the manner of medieval monsters, grotesques combine different parts of creatures with human parts and remain on a small scale. Here they have huge human ears, lions' manes, carnivore teeth and one has tiny hands coming out of its neck and another a bat's wings; the third is a man-figure just being rude. This mixing and matching of body parts has a very faint echo of classical monsters, like centaurs and sphinxes, manticores and mermaids and the

fear they engendered came from abnormal looks linked with abnormal powers. Some grotesques, such as those at Kilpeck Church in Herefordshire, were combined with other creatures indigenous to pre-Christian folklore, but our three are typical midlands gothic monsters. There were clergy efforts to suppress grotesques (seen as a flicker of paganism) which is why so many are high up in churches and so escaped Reformation destruction.

The combination of different body parts to create a fearful creature continued in the popular imagination until the nineteenth century, bypassing the age of reason, and having a final fling in the pages of William Blake. Then science took over with *Frankenstein* and *Dr Jekyll and Mr Hyde*, before the discovery of dinosaur parts and the acceptance of evolution to explain them, transformed the concept of monster into something huge and scaly. This new concept kept us on the edge of edge of our seats from Lewis Carroll's 'Jabberwocky' (a combination of dinosaur parts) via King Kong to Spielberg's *Jurassic Park* while Jaws qualified as a monster by being above average size and awfulness.

In the last decades, monsters have became space age, once again on a human scale but weird; think of ET who has transmogrified into fantasy Gollum in *The Lord of the Rings*. There have been efforts to reinstate size as in Ted Hughes 'Iron Man' but monsters today tend to the intergalactic eerie. Better not go out at night without a torch in Clifford Chambers. ◎◎

2 Accuracy

In 1965 the Women's Institute of Clifford Chambers entered the National Federation of Women's Institutes Jubilee Scrapbook Competition. The book, with its hessian cross-stitched embroidered cover is in the village archive and we selected some material, including these careful graphs showing village sanitation and occupations at that time. While these graphs look accurate, no information is given as to how data was gathered; was it a survey or is it from local government data? ◎◎

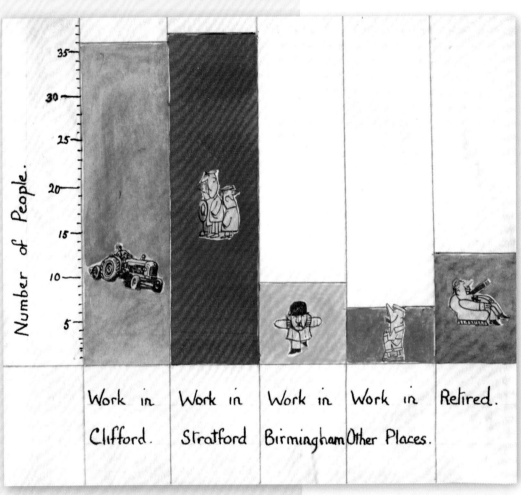

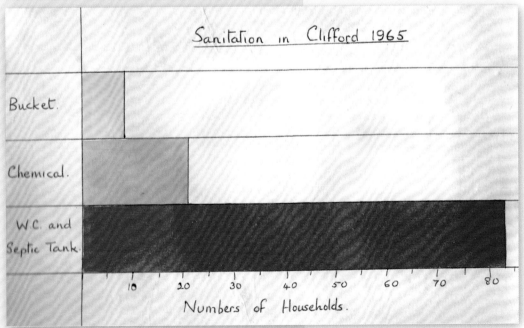

Clifford Chambers WI Golden Jubilee Scrapbook 1965 Village Archive

History According to A

3 Acquisition

This is about prices and values, income and lifestyle. Taken in 1977, this photograph shows no.33 and no.34 and the surrounding land. In 1951, when these two cottages were sold by the estate, no.33 was priced at £450 and no.34 at £280. Both then had outside bucket closets (down the garden of no.34 towards the river) and water from a pump outside no.32, but both had mains electricity. They are dated about 1860 and were cheaply built, walls being only one brick thick. Anecdote suggests they were the stables for the pub (no.28). In 1988 no.34 was bought at auction by a builder but its condition was so poor that the back wall fell down; the house was demolished, rebuilt and sold in 1991 for about £54,000, in part-exchange for a flat, the property market being by then depressed. In 2012 it sold for for £305,000 while no.33 was sold in 1996 for £62,000, two-thirds of it was then rebuilt and it is now valued at about £290,000.

By 1977, within the Square as a whole, the locally employed tenants had been replaced by homeowners, prices had risen and some professional people had begun to buy the properties which constituted the Square. The land was still unfenced, some vestiges of hedgerow remained and small-scale allotment crops were grown. Over the next thirty years, prices increased greatly and the escapist idyll of the country cottage took hold. Those with higher-paid jobs that necessitated absence and travel bought these and other Square properties. Because such homes represented such high outlay, the old deeds saying the attached land extended from the gooseberry bush to the pigsty were replaced with accurate measurements and deposited with the Land Registry; the land became defined with fences and gates marked 'private'.

Under tenancy ownership and open land, everyone knew everyone and, while there must have been neighbour disputes, there was no alternative but to rub along. Nowadays, with owners working long hours away and then coming home tired to costly, well-equipped houses and enclosed, private land, passing acknowledgement to the neighbours can suffice.

These Square properties now epitomise the country cottage in Shakespeare-land. They have all been restored to their peak and beyond it; granite kitchen work-tops, sand-blasted beams, carriage lamps, patio heaters, the lot. While some of them were at one time condemned as unfit for human habitation, they have not only been prevented from falling down but brought to the top of their market value. As usual with complex issues, the proportion of loss to benefit is undecided.
⊚⊚

Nos. 33 and 34 in 1977. Photograph lent by Charmian Evans

The same view 2013. Only the chimney of no. 33 can be seen

4 Affection

Three generations of the Wilks family have been married at St Helen's church

March 1955, John Wilks married Maisie Ulyatt

June 1978, Their son Phillip Wilks married Melanie Dallinger

June 2013, Their daughter Lindsey Wilks married Richard King

'Dearly beloved, we are gathered together here in the sight of God, and in the face of this congregation, to join together this Man and this Woman in holy Matrimony; which is an honourable estate, instituted of God in the time of man's innocency, signifying unto us the mystical union that is betwixt Christ and his Church; which holy estate Christ adorned and beautified by his presence, and first miracle that he wrought, in Cana of Galilee; and is commended of Saint Paul to be honourable among all men; and therefore is not by any to be enterprised, nor taken in hand, unadvisedly, lightly, or wantonly'. ◎◎

From the 'Solemnization of Matrimony' in *The Book of Common Prayer*. **Photographs lent by John and Philip Wilks**

5 Aggression

In this book, national events are mentioned only when they affected our parish. Such an event was the Battle of Evesham in 1265. It is important because it was one of many steps towards a national constitution that was to replace absolute kingship (over four centuries later) with parliament. Simon de Montfort challenged the power of Henry III (whose father, King John had signed the Magna Carter in 1215) and instigated the Provisions of Oxford, which was the first real attempt to establish a national constitution (which has still never been committed to

written confirmation). In the course of the following power struggle, the battle of Lewes in 1264 was a victory for de Montfort, and the humiliation of the king and loss of life was considerable.

The Battle of Evesham the next year was similarly ferocious and became an act of revenge by the king and his party against de Montfort, who was killed and mutilated. His army was decimated and the burial places of the thousands of dead became a matter of local legend.

In 1866, at Milcote in our parish, many skeletons were unearthed and this was written up in the 'Transactions' of the *Bristol and Gloucestershire Archaeological Society* in 1884/5 by R.F. Tomes, who made the following observation: 'If a distance of twelve or fourteen miles (from Evesham) were not too great, might not the thousands of skeletons which lie buried at Milcote and only a little way from one of the fords of the Avon, be those of the flying multitudes escaping from the Battle of Evesham? Such a suggestion was indeed made in 1866 when a great many of those remains were exhumed and their crania found to be those of mixed race, like the English of the present day and more especially when it was discovered that the skeletons were men in the prime of life, and men of considerable stature. As I saw some hundreds exposed, at this remarkable burying place, I can distinctly state that such was the case.' ◎◎

6 Agony and adoration

The War Memorial in the Square is attributed to Ninian Comper who was one of the last pure Gothic pastiche ecclesiastical designers. His work blends invisibly into the fabric of Westminster Abbey and many other churches. Unequivocally in the tradition of renaissance sculpture, the figures are vigorous and expressive. Dedicated in 1919 for those who fell in the First World War, the lettering had to be extended later to include those who died in the Second World War.

At the top is Christ on the cross with Mary his mother and also the beloved disciple, St John to whom he said, "Behold thy mother! "And from that hour the disciple took her into his own home'. (John 19.26). St John is traditionally shown beardless and with curly hair.

This is the same disciple who leant against Jesus' breast at the Last Supper, the one who heard his heart beating, the one whom Jesus loved (John 13.23). He is also understood to be the author of John's gospel where we find the verse that is quoted on war memorials up and down the land: 'Greater love hath no man than this, that a man lay down his life for his friends' (John 15.13).

For Christians the crucifixion of Jesus is central to their faith and understanding of God. It is Christian belief that Jesus was not only mortal but the son of God, and therefore divine and his mortal death was a confirmation that God is present in the whole of human experience. Since it is also believed that Jesus rose from the dead, the cross represents the core belief of Christianity that death is not the end of personal existence. It also reminds Christians that suffering is part of being human and that God has shared and participated in this as a mortal man.

The Emperor Constantine, son of St Helen, banned crucifixion throughout the Roman Empire on his conversion to Christianity in 311, in honour of Jesus. ◎◎

7 Agriculture

The 1965 Women's Institute Scrapbook included this map which shows (nearly all) of the parish and the crops grown at that time. Crops grown nearby nowadays are restricted to barley, oats and wheat, oil-seed rape, runner beans and stick beans, besides salad onions and salad crops. The land used to be harvested by local labour, and now immigrant people, who either live here or who visit seasonally, are employed on the harvest. Poles, Latvians, Iraqis, French, Croatians and Pakistanis have all been harvesting here in the last few years. ◎◎

Clifford Chambers WI Golden Jubilee Scrapbook 1965 Village Archive

8 Altercation

The most valuable and intriguing of St Helen's possessions are the silver gilt chalice and paten, which have been in the church's ownership since around 1780. They are valuable because of their date and rare because of their desecration. Equally intriguing is the fact that, until recently when their considerable value was recognised, the chalice and paten were in regular use at communion services, and members of the congregation would take them home to clean.

They were left to Lister Dighton, lord of the manor of Clifford Chambers, in the will of Alice Dormer of Ascott Park in Oxfordshire, whereupon he bequeathed them to the church in about 1780.

Photograph of desecrating lettering

These two pieces, dating from 1494/5, are the second oldest hallmarked examples of church plate in England. The hallmarks are the same on both, indicating that they were the work of the same silversmith and were made in the same year. The marks are as follows: first a crowned leopard's head, with the crown being of the earliest type and the leopard indicating that they were made in London; second a Gothic capital R which is the date letter for 1494/5; and finally an eagle's or a vulture's head, the maker's mark.

Patens survived the depredations of the Reformation more frequently than chalices, but it is remarkable that these two pieces, which seem either to have been made to go with each other or were purchased at the same time, have not only both survived but have stayed together for the entire six hundred years since they were created.

The circular silver paten is simpler in form and design than its more ornate companion. Its shallow bowl has been beaten into two hexagonal scallop-shaped rings, the outer one delicately ornamented. In the centre is a vernicle, the face of Christ miraculously transposed onto the cloth with which Veronica wiped his face on his way to Calvary. Christ's head has a halo behind it with a fleur-de-lis, and the background is slightly hatched, but perhaps not deeply enough to indicate enamelling.

The bowl of the chalice has a round bottom with the sides continuing straight up into a cone shape. A hexagonal shaft leads down to a hexagonal splayed star-shaped foot, with each point of the star ending in a small crescent. One face on the foot is carved with a crucifix with a piece of foliage in each bottom angle; the ground behind the figure is roughly hatched, which may indicate that it was enamelled. Halfway between the foot and the bowl is a hexagonal 'pommel' or 'node' with six diamond-shaped lozenges spaced around it, five of them carved with a letter of the name IESUS and the sixth with a cross in the form of a *croix pattée*, (a cross with equal length arms narrow at the centre and broader at the edge). Small indents on the pommel indicate that it may originally have been set with stones, probably cabochon-cut semi-precious gems such as agates or carnelians. The lozenges appear to have been originally filled with enamel.

The stem and the pommel, the mouldings at the edge of the foot and the crescents are gilt, as are the crucifixion and its accompanying foliage as well as the inside of the bowl, with the gilding extending over the brim. The rest of the chalice is silver and carries an additional fascinating feature; a curse which has been scratched onto the six lozenges surrounding the pommel. The chalice has to be turned upside down to see these little marks, which read – starting from the S of Jesus's name and ending at the cross – A POX ON Y (ye).

Professor Ronnie Mulryne, writing in *Trinity Times* (Holy Trinity's parish magazine, February 2012), speculates on a possible perpetrator. It seems that John Dormer, husband of Alice Dormer, who bequeathed the chalice to Lister Dighton, was a reprobate, described by the eighteenth-century antiquarian Thomas Hearne as 'a young gentleman of a most wicked, profligate, debauch'd life, a person of no conscience nor religion, and who is not known to have ever done one virtuous or good thing… a sad swearing heathenish irreligious man'. He murdered a man in Woodstock Park 'because he would not hand over his wife for Dormer's gratification' and escaped hanging for the crime because one of his judges was also a Dormer. It is presumed that the chalice and paten were part of his or his wife's family church plate, and it seems more than possible that it was this loutish anti-religious philistine who desecrated the sacred vessel by inverting the name of Jesus and scratching his rough curse next to it. He died of smallpox at the age of forty, which if he was the author of the curse seems altogether appropriate.

Lister Dighton apparently bequeathed them to St Helen's, where they were used for holy communion until 2010, when their value was realised. They are now on loan and displayed at Compton Verney, Warwickshire. ◉◎

9 Alteration

Safely tucked away in St Helen's vestry with piles of defunct hymn books and flower vases, is a large prayer book entitled *The Book of Common Prayer and administration of the sacraments and other rites and ceremonies according to the uses of the Church Of England*. Oxford, printers to the University 1799. Price 17s unbound.'

In 1799 George III was king and the Revd Arthur Annesley was rector at St Helen's. He served until 1845 throughout the reigns of George IV and William IV and into the reign of Queen Victoria. He must therefore have been responsible for the careful alterations of this prayer book whereby the name of the previous monarch has been carefully pasted over with printed corrections, cut out with scissors and neatly inserted. On the next page, the alterations include reference to Queen Adelaide, Queen Victoria's aunt (widow of William IV) so this careful pasting must date from before 1849 when she died.

While this prayer book was printed in 1799, it is the same in content as was adopted by the Church of England in 1662 on the restoration of the monarch (apart from changes in the name of the sovereign). This remained in use unaltered until 1927/8 when a newer version was prepared and in 2000, Common Worship was offered to all churches.

As with the Bible, the prayer book was put together during the stop-and-start process of the English Reformation with the aim of conducting the state religion in the English language. Both the Bible and the prayer book were conceived during the Henry VIII Reformation, were consolidated under Archbishop Cranmer during the reign of Edward V and then suffered a brutal rejection by Queen Mary, who burnt Cranmer publicly at Oxford. They were redeemed by Queen Elizabeth, given polished lingual form and political prominence by James I, suffered under the Civil Wars, but were both rescued after the restoration of Charles II and remained largely unaltered for over two centuries.

While the Bible is the narrative that forms the basis of the Christian religion, the prayer book is the workshop of it, giving a form to the services of worship to the God described by the Bible. It includes the morning and evening services of prayer, the communion service and occasional services besides the rites for baptism, marriage and burial; it also specifies what parts of the Bible are to be read throughout the church year. It is thorough, mystical yet practical and set a pattern of church services that has lasted. This is one reason that a church like St Helen's did not need to renew the big master prayer book once 17s. had been spent on its purchase, except to neatly alter the prayer for the sovereign from 'our most gracious Sovereign Lord, King George' to 'our most gracious Sovereign Lady, Queen Victoria'. ◎◎

10 Amnesia

Sometimes the provenance and purpose of an item can become completely forgotten. At some point during the tenure of the Revd Pippet (1895–1918) there was found in a cupboard at St Helen's a fine, large, gilt-lace edged velvet cloth and a similar cushion. He photographed these and, for some time, the cloth was used as an alter frontal.

Village tradition believed that it was used at the funeral of Catherine of Aragon because it apparently featured her emblem, embroidered pomegranates. It was loaned to Warwickshire County Museums and in 1982 examined by Santina Levey, Keeper of Textiles at the Victoria and Albert Museum. She concluded that the cloth was a bearing cloth on which a child was carried at its christening and only used by those of gentry status and above. The cloth is silk velvet, probably Italian, and the border of gold and silver lace was probably made in London. It is a rare survival because of the value of the precious metals used and is dated about 1675. Also considered was the cushion on which the lace was identified as being of domestic design, and dates from between 1625 and 1635.

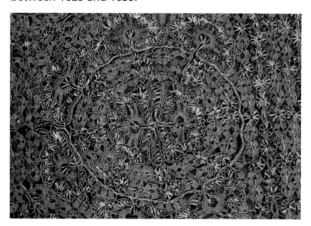

A bearing cloth could traditionally indicate the status of a child:

'Look thee, a bearing cloth for a squire's child.'
Winter's Tale 3 iv 112

We might wonder how such precious items came to be in a cupboard at St Helen's. One speculation is that the cushion might have been given to the church at the time of the Civil War in the mid-seventeenth century when the last Rainsford to live at the manor was forced to sell his birthright and flee because of his ardent royalism. The origin of the bearing cloth remains a mystery but it may well have come from the manor. ◎◎

A Prayer for the King's Majesty.

O Lord our heavenly Father, high and mighty, King of kings, Lord of lords, the only Ruler of princes, who doſt from thy throne behold all the dwellers upon earth; Moſt heartily we beſeech thee with thy favour to behold our moſt gracious Sovereign **Lady Queen Victoria,** ; and ſo repleniſh **her** with the grace of thy Holy Spirit, that **she** may alway incline to thy will, and walk in thy way: Endue **her** plenteouſly with heavenly gifts; grant **her** in health and wealth long to live; ſtrengthen **her** that **she** may vanquiſh and overcome all **her** enemies; and finally, after this life, **she** may attain everlaſting joy and felicity; through Jeſus Chriſt our Lord. *Amen.*

11 Anger

This must be one of the most famous recorded episodes of a loss of temper.

'And the Jews' passover was at hand and Jesus went up to Jerusalem. And found in the temple those that sold oxen and sheep and doves, and the changers of money sitting: And when he had made a scourge of small cords, he drove them all out of the temple, and the sheep, and the oxen; and poured out the changers' money, and overthrew the tables; And he said unto them that sold doves, Take these things hence; make not my Father's house an house of merchandise.' (John 2. 12-16)

The splendid red-robed figure of Jesus is from the right-hand light of the window in the chancel east end at St Helen's. It was designed and made by a London based firm, T.F. Curtis Wood and Hughes who were highly accomplished makers of ecclesiastical stained glass from the mid-nineteenth to the early twentieth century. Their work is pastiche Italian renaissance, echoing the intricate decorative figures of Carlo Crivelli but, at its best, is full of narrative and very well painted. This firm made windows for Gloucester, Lincoln and Lichfield cathedrals and Holy Trinity in Stratford also has fine windows from their studio.

The Revd Pippet, who commissioned this in memory of his parents in 1899, clearly had discriminating taste. This is a 'top of the range' commission by a nationally known firm, as was his commission of the war memorial by Ninian Comper, also a well accredited figure in his field. Neither commission was modern in the terms of the day, both are conventional pastiche pieces but lovely and of the highest quality carving, drawing and colouration, which is perhaps appropriate for a little place like Clifford Chambers.

This is an unusual subject from the gospels and, particularly at this period, depictions are rare. It could be questioned whether there was a banking crisis at the time or whether the Revd Pippet had any issue with the banks to justify this depiction.

12 Anguish

It is all too clear from so many of St Helen's gravestones that in the past life expectancy for the majority was limited to what today we would count as early middle age, and that death was no respecter of wealth or position.

But then, as now, and even though for infants survival was even more of a lottery, the loss of a child or children was grievous indeed. The parish records show that even the wealthy Rainsfords from the manor suffered the early deaths of several of their children in every generation, and the brass of Elizabeth Marrowe (née Rainsford) in the church records not only her death in childbirth but that of her newborn daughter too. John and Ada Silvester buried one son at the age of eight and another who lived a mere sixteen days. James and Mary Ann Nason had two children who both died in infancy. The inscription of 1821 on the children's grave is poignant; the stone is almost illegible today.

Thy parents grieve to be thus parted
But comfort they may take in weeping
For he who heals the broken hearted
Whispers they babes are in my keeping

Even for those who survived childhood life could often be brief, cut short by illness or accident. Reginald Annesley, the son of the vicar, died suddenly aged seventeen in 1882. William Garner was twenty-three when he was killed on the railway in 1872 and his twin brother Thomas died too only a couple of years later. John Rouse, aged twenty-six in 1851, had already lost both his parents and then that year suffered the death of his younger brother William, aged twelve; perhaps it is not surprising that he survived him by a matter of months. And then there is John Parry Nash, Surgeon 'whose skill in that profession prolonged the life of others'. He died in 1816 at twenty-nine and is grandly memorialised in the church by his parents who mourned their only son as one 'whose life was the chief solace of their own'. This fine early eighteenth-century carved marble wall plaque denoted class in its quality, style, placing and prose. The rubbing below is of the bottom ten lines. ◎◎

13 Animals

Until recent times, farm animals such as chickens, cows, pigs, sheep and horses were kept extensively as the local economy depended on them. Nowadays, memories of the last pig in the village are as nostalgic as memories of the last porter seen on Stratford station. Wild animals are listed in Stefan Buczacki's chapter but they are only rarely seen. In the snow, footprints show what is around and this includes what are probably muntjac deer which wander across the Square's land, but fences now restrict their movement.

During farming days, everyone was close to animals in their various stages of life and death. Goats, chickens, dogs and cats roamed and evidence of slaughter was apparent; bone yards were turned once a week for the chickens to gorge on the maggots. Killing of animals was accepted, but this did not negate affection and respect; once a dog was past an active life, if it was respected it was shot, if not, it was drowned to save the bullet. Chickens are having a revival, but dogs that are pets are the most ubiquitous animal here today. ◎◎

Yet why should Friendship mourn his early doom
Or why Parental Love weep o'er the Tomb
Of one, from Virtues paths too good to stray
Whose home is Heav'n—whose light, eternal day?
For thus *RELIGION* softly whispers Peace,
And bids the Sorrows of the Mourner cease—
—Live as he Liv'd—the ways of God to scan
Die, as he died—in peace with Him, and Man
Walk in the pure, the sacred, path He trod
And share with Him the *PARADISE* of God

Wax-crayon rubbing of the Nash memorial in the chancel: made 2013

Sow and its breeder in front of the rectory, 1963
English Heritage Archive

14 Anniversary

A union jack was flown in the Square for the Jubilee and Olympic celebrations in June 2012. The photograph below was taken through the Church vestry window through panes of glass that may have been taken from a fourteenth-century window demolished in the nave when it was moved from its present position during the late nineteenth-century reconstructions.

There has always been an England
An older England still,
Where Chaucer rode to Canterbury
And Falstaff drank his fill.

Where poets scrawled immortal lines
Beside a daffodil,
And lovers lay upon the grass
Atop of Bredon Hill.

Where parson in his pulpit droned
As Nancy winked at Bill,
Where Brontës conjured moonlit paths
And Hardy drowned a mill.

Where jolly tars sailed hearts-of-oak
From China to Brazil,
And foxes sought out Squire's pack
To race them for the thrill.

We never could cease worshipping
What never was – nor will:
There has always been an England
An older England still.

Felix Dennis, *Tales from the Woods*, 2010
☺

15 Apathy

Porch door of St Helen's showing the fifteenth-century chuch door

Henry and Margaret were buying an old church.
Henry said it had a Wow factor.
He liked it more than he could say.
He could put his computer in the old chancel, was it?
The staircases were top spec. Fantastic floors.
Margaret was not put off by the graveyard at all
And certainly could do something with it
To make it match up to their requirements.
She could just see her guests gazing up to where
The architect had put the granny flat
While preserving the pulpit as conversation piece.
The font was wittily converted to a shower
And in the mezzanine stained glass at knee level
was a definite plus.
The leper hole made a convenient serving hatch.
The only problem was: it was a semi.
You could either own the tower or the graveyard.
Tough choice: or could they stretch to both?
Miles Burrows, 'The Curfew Tolls', *Times Literary Supplement*, July 2013 ✑✑

16 Apparel

The huge hats the girls are wearing were popular before the First World War. Clothes were a major economic demand for the parents of children like these. Older sisters would have been servant girls. 'Their print morning dresses were pretty, lilac, or pink or buff, sprigged with white which were cut down for the little girls to wear on May Day and for churchgoing throughout the summer..... Devotion to fashion gave a spice to life and helped to make bearable the underlying poverty. But the poverty was there... one might have a velvet tippet but no shoes worth mentioning' (Flora Thompson, *Lark Rise to Candleford*)

All the children wear hats or caps, partly for warmth and because hair was probably only washed in the weekly bath night with hard soap; scalp condition such as ringworm could be concealed under caps. These tough little boys would soon be fodder for Flanders fields.

The two cotton-print aprons below were found in a skip in the Square in the late 1990s. They belonged to Phyllis Salmon who apparently was a hoarder, which may explain why they had never been used. The fabric design dates them to the 1930s and the price tag on the purple and blue apron is two shillings and eleven pence, and that on the green apron is one shilling and ninepence half-penny. ✑✑

May Day celebrations, before 1905

Harvest supper in the Village Hall, October 2012. Photograph: Myles Pollock

17 Appetite

We may live without poetry, music and art;
We may live without conscience and live without art;
We may live without friends, we may live without
 books;
But civilised man cannot live without cooks.
He may live without books, what is knowledge but
 grieving?
He may live without hope, what is hope but deceiving?
He may live without love, what is passion but pining?
But where is a man that can live without dining?

Owen Meredith (1831-1891) ◉◉

A History According to A

18 Arboreal angularity

We stated in our Introduction that material about the rectory is not included simply for reasons of space. A detailed architectural and archival study has been made of it by Nat Alcock (who has researched and written our chapter on the Square's properties); this included detailed dendrochronological analysis of beam samples, which has given the date of the felling of the trees used to build it as the winter of 1433/4. It is probable that the house was built in the summer of 1434 and close structural examination of the house also implies that the whole house is of this date.

It was built by the then rector, John Bokeland (whom we discuss briefly in our church chapter). It is a rectory rather than a vicarage because the incumbent was entitled to all the tithes, or the 'great tithes' of the land's produce, rather than just the 'smaller tithes' or a salary which was due to a vicar; it also owned land and was one of the most valuable holdings in the diocese. John Bokeland was an ecclesiastic of some significance and of the list of forty-three rectors listed in the church, they include a dean of Hereford Cathedral and a president of Magdalen College in Oxford. Few of these rectors would have lived here and the work of the parish would have been carried out by a succession of curates who would have lived in a part of the rectory, of whom little is known although research has revealed many of their names and dates of service.

The house consists of a classic 'hall and cross-wing' plan, typical of medieval farmhouses and lesser manor houses, and it was built with monied care. The central section comprises a two-bay hall which would have extended upwards into much of the roof area but which is now ceilinged with a corridor and two rooms above. The cross-wings both extend forward on the south side, giving it a splendid entrance facade and the western of these wings gave a single fine room on two floors with stone fireplaces. The east wing was partitioned to give two rooms on each floor.

Some alterations have been made over the centuries but its original structure, layout and purpose are all apparent. It was subdivided in the early nineteenth century and used by curates and tenants until the twentieth century. It went into private ownership in 1982 and has been subsequently restored, handled and studied in a knowledgeable and careful manner. ◎◎

19 Armorial ancestry

This latten brass shows three unidentified young girls, 'maydens' implied by the loose hair. It is a detached fragment from the memorial brass to Elizabeth Rainsford who married Edward Marrowe and who died in childbirth in 1601, aged twenty. Her brass as a single detached figure is on the chancel wall. This latten fragment was painted white at some time and has been roughly cleaned.

We have paired this with a photograph of Jesse Snow and her cousin Grace Williams, taken at Christmas 1995 at no.34.

Life expectancy for women in 1601 was about 35. Current UK estimates from the Office for National Statistics at birth are 82.3 years for women and 78.2 years for men. ◎◎

The medieval rectory adjacent to the church

Lent by the Snow family.

20 Artisan artefacts or 'ammers and 'ooves'

These eight hammers as used by a fireman, coal-man, carpenter and cobbler, were retrieved from a skip in the Square in the late 1990s. All these trades were apparently practised nearby, probably until the Second World War. Also included are four horse and donkey shoes dug up in the garden of no.33 which anecdotally was said to have been a stable for the pub's horses; the presence of these iron shoes may corroborate this. They have been photographed on what may have been their stable floor which is laid in slabs of Jurassic lias. This is known locally as 'Wilmcote stone' as it was quarried at nearby Wilmcote, both the canal and railway line in the eighteenth and nineteenth centuries being routed through Wilmcote for the purpose of transporting it. The last quarry closed in the early twentieth century. @@

21 Artistry

In 1970 there was an exhibition held at the Shakespeare Centre in Henley Street of the work of a local artist, William Wells Quatremain (1857–1930). He was a watercolour painter of small-scale townscapes of Stratford and rural scenes in the villages nearby and, for this occasion, two hundred pictures were identified and nearly seventy exhibited.

He appears to have been a shy man and to have earned his living mainly as a bookseller. As an artist, he was apparently self-taught, but he married the widow of his neighbour, J.T. Marshall, who was an artist and teacher of watercolour painting so perhaps this was his instruction and influence. Certainly his work does not imply amateurism in any sense and he is a typical, late Victorian accomplished painter of town and country tranquillity.

He had two important patrons, one of whom was Frances, Countess of Warwick and the other was Marie Corelli who wrote about him in 1903 in her magazine *The Avon Star*. 'He was an extremely unpretentious man, working at his art always with the greatest love for it, and with an extreme pride and tenderness in the faithful rendering of such 'old' bits of Stratford and the surrounding neighbourhood as may best present them to the heart, mind and memory.'

He is now becoming collectable, partly because he produced a lot of identifiable work and also because he has not until recently been expensive to buy. However, as in this picture of Clifford Chambers rectory and church, he shows a scene that could be a hundred years earlier which accords with many people's desire to view the past through rose-tinted spectacles. @@

Painting lent by a private collector

22 Association

Clifford's church is dedicated to St Helen and, while we do not know why our church has such an association, we discuss possible reasons in our chapter on the church. In 2012, the Hosking Houses Trust invited Marina Warner, their patron, to give a talk in the church about the myth and history of St Helen; some of her material is included here.

There is no doubt that Helena was a real person; the wife of one Roman emperor, Constantius (who died in 306) and the mother of another, Constantine. It also appears to be true that she lived to a great age, and towards the end of her life visited Palestine where she founded churches and hunted for relics associated with Jesus.

We say 'appears to be true' because there are ancient sources for her history which can almost certainly be relied on for at least some aspects of the reality of her life. The near contemporary historian Eusebius states that she was around eighty when she undertook the journey to Palestine, which from other sources is datable to the mid-320s AD. She is likely to have been born sometime between 240 and 250, probably in a village called Drepanum in Bithynia, part of modern Turkey, and apparently to a family of innkeepers. She may have met Constantius, who was the nephew of the emperor, when he was campaigning in the region, and it is not clear whether she was legally married to him or maintained as his mistress. One of the sources for her life uses both 'wife' and 'concubine' to describe her relationship with him. She was with him, however, for some twenty years and was the mother of his only son, Constantine. When Constantius became emperor, he put Helena aside in favour of a more noble bride, and she lived in obscurity for some fourteen years until his death. After the accession of her son, she was summoned back to court and showered with wealth and honours.

When Constantine embraced Christianity in 311, after seeing a vision before his victory at the battle of the Milvian Bridge of a cross superimposed on the sun with the words 'in hoc signo vinces', 'under this sign you will conquer', his mother too became a devout Christian. Her pilgrimage to the Middle East saw her arriving with lavish gifts from her son which she intended to use to do honour to the sacred places associated with the life of Jesus. Although she is believed to have dressed simply and loved to mingle anonymously with the ordinary worshippers at church, Helena heaped munificent gifts on all the churches she visited, and founded two new ones: the church of the Nativity at Bethlehem above the cave which was traditionally believed to be the place of Jesus' birth; and a church on the Mount of Olives to commemorate the Ascension.

She was apparently determined to find the cross on which Jesus had been crucified, and she is reputed to have succeeded when workmen were demolishing Hadrian's Temple of Venus on the hill of Calvary, or Golgotha, before beginning the construction of what was to be Constantine's basilica of the Holy Sepulchre. Three crosses and some nails were discovered under the foundations of the temple, along with the placard proclaiming: 'This was the king of the Jews'. But it was not clear which cross was

the right one. Accordingly, Helena brought to the place a woman in the last stages of leprosy, who touched each cross in turn. When she touched the true one, her lesions fell away and her disease was cured. Constantine later incorporated one of the nails into his horse's bridle and the other into his helmet.

Her discovery of the cross is not in fact mentioned by any contemporary historians, but within a century of her death Helena was being credited with it. She died around AD 330 and was buried with great pomp by Constantine; her sarcophagus is in the Vatican Museum in Rome.

There is, however, an alternative narrative of St Helen's life. In the Middle Ages Henry of Huntingdon and Geoffrey of Monmouth dreamed up a mythical British origin for Helen, as the daughter of Coel, a British king who was supposed to have founded Colchester; her connection with that city is still enshrined in its arms which

Folio of the frescoes of the Guild Chapel entitled, *A Series of Ancient Allegorical Historical and Legendary Paintings*, which were discovered in the summer of 1804 on the walls of the Chapel of the Trinity (belonging to the Guild of the Holy Cross) at Stratford-up-Avon, Warwickshire

From Drawings made at the time of their discovery by Thomas Fisher FSA, Published 1836

By permission of The Shakespeare Birthplace Trust

she recovered, verifying its authenticity. This panel was from the north wall of the chancel, in the lower tier. The paintings faded and vanished soon after their discovery.

St Helen's would have had frescoes much like this before the Reformation. ◎/◎

23 Attainment

Two people of significant artistic attainment are associated with Clifford Chambers; one is Michael Drayton to whom we devote a whole chapter, and the other is Tibor Reich (1916–1996) who was a designer of printed and woven textiles.

Stefan Buczacki mentions in his chapter about the River Stour that there were two mills, the lower mill being adjacent to the main road from Stratford. It ceased being used for milling in the 1920s and was later adapted for commercial and light industrial work, Tibor Reich setting up both his home and his business there in 1945.

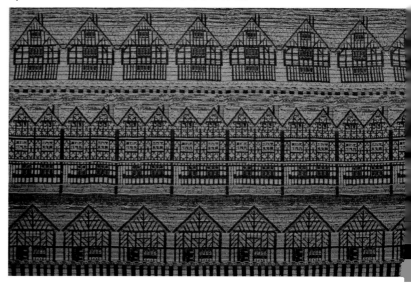

carry a cross and nails with three crowns. Very beautiful and skilled in music and the arts, she was married to Constantius through a treaty between her father and the Roman general.

The picture we show above is a nineteenth-century engraving by the antiquarian Thomas Fisher (1781-1836) of one of the frescoes that were uncovered in the Guild Chapel at Stratford-upon-Avon. They had been commissioned in the late-fourteenth or early-fifteenth century by the Guild of the Holy Cross and consisted of several large panels showing the life of St Helen. Late in the process of the Reformation, they were limewashed out of sight in 1563 and were not uncovered until 1804, when the antiquarian Thomas Fisher made a series of detailed engravings of them. This one we have chosen shows 'The testing of the Cross' whereby St Helen lays the cross she had discovered against a dying woman, and

Born in Budapest, Tibor's father was the manufacturer of ribbons used in Hungarian peasant costumes and also braids for the military. He loved their brilliant colours woven into tight patterns, but the second great influence upon him was the German Bauhaus, the modern movement of the 1930s, where everything was abstract and simplified with clear colours and basic shapes. Bringing these double influences to England, he trained at Leeds University in textile manufacture and set up his business in the village.

In 1945, wartime rationing of materials meant that the design and manufacturing of textiles specified how much yarn could be used per square foot, how much dye and patterns had to be reversible. Bringing together his memories of patterned braids and his understanding of Europe's modern art movement, Tibor's weaving looms (converted from five broken

Arden Tapestry, A woven fabric by Tibor Reich based upon half-timbered local buildings. A variety of yarns were used for the background and the images of the timbered buildings were interwoven by hand-operated Jacquard machine.

By permission of The Shakespeare Birthplace Trust and of the Reich family

down hand looms) produced textured abstract fabrics with typical names like 'diaper' and 'zigzag'. By the 1950s he was also designing printed fabrics using photographic enlargements of leaves and water (lots of both around the Mill) and designing pottery and carpets in the post-war, Festival of Britain enthusiasm for new homes and new fashions.

Recognition, awards and commissions were won internationally, of which the best remembered locally is the Stratford Memorial Theatre refurbishment of 1952 for which he designed all the fabrics. He also contributed to the Shakespeare Birthplace Trust's new building in the 1960s, which still has some of his curtaining in its original position.

Tibor left the Mill in 1978 because of the continual risk of flooding and designed and built a house for himself and his family, one of Stratford's few modern houses, in Avenue Road. He died in 1996. ◎◎

24 Attendance

The reasons for church attendance have varied over time but these are perhaps the most obvious:

'Some of them went to church to show off their best clothes and to see and criticise those of their neighbours; some because they loved to hear their own voices raised in the hymns, or because the churchgoing qualified them for the Christmas blankets and coals; and a few to worship.'

Flora Thompson, *Lark Rise to Candleford*

Spiritual conviction

The practice of faith by worshipping a personal God, 'Maker of all things, judge of all men' (from the General Confession in *The Book of Common Prayer*). The reported gains are an indefinable inner peace satisfying an internal desire to conduct a personal life beyond obvious worldly needs, by adherence to the basic tenets of Christianity which are love, morality and service and that death is a process, not a completion.

Psychological reassurance

Stemming from forgiveness of failure and the promise of a new start each week. 'Forgive us all that is past, And grant that we may ever hereafter serve and please thee in newness of life', says *The Book of Common Prayer* and again, in an invitation to confession; 'If we say we have no sin, we deceive ourselves and the truth is not in us; If we confess our sins, God is faithful and just to forgive us our sins, and cleanse us from all unrighteousness'. It makes a good start to the week.

Social requirement

Church attendance was for centuries the self-evident glue that held society together. Then as now, it encouraged neighbour approval and established that, at least to all appearances, your neighbours held the same values as yourself. Unfortunately, though, the church in England has also perpetuated a cultural hierarchy. The buildings themselves often emanate a sense of everyone knowing their place. Hence 'good Anglicans' tend not to fill up the pews from the front, leaving them empty in case someone more important than themselves turns up.

Community cohesion

The activities associated with dressing and serving the church are many and varied, involve lots of people who share these values. There was music to play and sing, the Sunday school and all the many associated activities, the church being the focus of processions and events.

Family reasons

The morality of Christianity was the structure for family life through baptism, marriage and burial and these three ceremonies persist. In marrying, the human potential for love and commitment is celebrated in that union; in burying, by committing a dead person's body to the earth and in giving thanks for that life. Although cremation takes place at a crematorium, ashes are often interred in the consecrated churchyard.

Stability and comfort

The church was and is usually a large building which, with its clock and bells, its regular services and presumed responsibilities to every individual, may have been oppressive but was reliable. 'Stands the church clock at ten to three, and is there honey still for tea?' ('Grantchester', Rupert Brooke). 'Stability' too is a great watchword of the Benedictine monastic tradition, the most prominent kind of religious life in Europe, having been authorised by Emperor Charlemagne. The comforting repetition of liturgy which forms the bedrock of worship in the Anglican and Catholic traditions owes much to the speaking and singing of the offices.

Sex

Church is where men and women could meet and see each other at their most attractive, tidied up and wearing their Sunday best, and have a quiet time to study each other. Whatever happened all week, you could see where everybody was on Sunday. In the novel *How Far Can You Go?* by David Lodge, he takes nine young people and the priest at an early morning Catholic service and considers their motives. Sex is a powerful motive, and anyone, almost anyone, however scrofulous, adolescent or inadequate looks handsomer in a white ruff or a dog collar. Flowing vestments, with a passing glance to the shape of monastic habits, are intended to eschew sexual attractiveness, but like anything in life can be customised and made to suit all tastes. How much lace, if any, is in the trimmings? How fitted are the waist and bust?

Sex might be a less obvious reason for church attendance today, as there are many more opportunities for people, and especially young people, to meet each other. Congregations are today tending to be elderly and consist mainly of women.

Historical continuity

The words of the common mass go back to the second century, and some churches (including St Helen's) have existed for a thousand years. This endurance is comforting, especially during uncertain times. We are sitting in the pews and walking down the aisles, and blinking into the sun at the church door with the generations who have gone before. This is one of the things Christianity means when in the creed it affirms 'the communion of saints.'

St Helen's facing east, Easter, 1901

St.Helen's facing west, 2013

Fear

Christianity holds many promises but also threats and warnings of after-life retribution. Religious practice can be a form of after-life insurance. Comfort and defence in the apparent presence of witchcraft and hauntings are still the role of the church. Witchcraft is frightening because it seeks to control events and people to usually (but not always) malevolent ends. Spells and prayers are worlds apart. Spells seek to invoke action, prayers express desire ('Give us this day our daily bread') or are a petition ('Forgive us our trespasses as we forgive those who trespass against us'). When needed (and this does occur in contemporary society) a priest can be called on to be a watchman and to act in defence of his or her people.

Law

It was for centuries a legal requirement to attend church at least once a year. Church attendance was widely believed to be God's law and so was given statute. This means of social control by the state was not repealed until the 1820s by a Liberal government, but it had not been enforced for some considerable time and had fallen into disrepute. Catholics were emancipated from their banishment of holding public office in 1829 although again this had not been enforced. In a rural area such as this, it would have been an obligation for the workers to attend church and the same church as their master (if he was a Catholic or a Methodist, so were they). The manor owner here at Clifford as elsewhere would have paid for much of the church's upkeep; also, all the houses here were owned by the manor whose owners were almost the sole employers for the area. Within memory, Mrs Douty could prevent the children from playing on a Sunday because she expected them to be in church so, while it was not always a legal demand, it was certainly an unavoidable obligation.

Aesthetic and learning

The church has been, even beyond the demands of the state or the individual, the greatest commissioner, inspirer and enabler of the arts and associated professions in our world-wide culture. There are things to see and listen to in a church of enduring content and cultural importance.

Cultural paucity: there was nothing else to do on the one day of the week designated by law a holiday, there was no other entertainment including music, teaching, excitement, colour or stories. Some people say that attendance at church declined so heavily when *The Forsyte Saga* was being shown on television (a sort of 1960s equivalent of *Downton Abbey*) that it more or less killed Evensong.

Reasons for non-attendance are easier to identify: Post Christian secularism

For such we must call it, whether we wish to or not. If ever a little village like Clifford Chambers decides it no longer wants to keep its church operating for worship, what happens to it?

Either a church is amalgamated with another parish but since this has probably already been done (as with St Helen's) this simply further dilutes church leadership. Or the chancel may be retained for occasional worship and the rest converted for other uses (a youth centre, a café, a shop) or the whole building is de-consecrated and sold for private housing (as at Atherstone, the neighbouring village). We deal further with this issue under 'A for Apathy' page 58.

Effect of two world wars

These wars touched every community in the nation, and led to a disenchantment with a God whom many people blamed for allowing so much loss of life. There was after both wars a rise in spiritualism but not spirituality.

Rise of rationality

The concept of God has lost near universal acceptance because, from the beginning of belief, anything that could not be understood could be ascribed to God. That included everything from earth and sky, natural surroundings (storms and rainbows), birth, welfare in life and death. Nowadays, we are attended and comforted physically in life, death and illness like never before in history and no longer need to cling to superstition. As understanding improved, especially in the Age of Enlightenment and its emphasis on deepening scientific and philosophical enquiry, God began to be relegated. Once the planetary system and space began to be further understood, God diminished further until, in our present age of amazing analysis and conclusions, God for many people has no apparent role.

Personal loss

We have mentioned David Lodge's novel *How far Can You Go?* in which one couple lose a daughter and subsequently their faith at the pointlessness of the death. Such trauma on a personal or greater level can reinforce, or destroy a personal faith.

Distractions elsewhere

Modern society offers so many distractions that are more fun, including sport, culture and travel. Sundays are now a time for shopping, D.I.Y., washing the car, gardening and sleeping in.

Mobility of society

The general mobility of people discourages a consistent, committed involvement with the church.

Interest in other religions

Better education and a multi-faith society can offer alternative spiritual paths, and knowledge and interest in other faiths can sometimes appear to compete against Christianity. Of course, there are some truths and attitudes which resonate across all religions. Christianity is distinctive because of its faith in the Incarnation (God becoming a human being in the person of Jesus who was entirely human and entirely divine, celebrated at Christmas) and the Resurrection (that God through Jesus put an end to death by rising from the dead, celebrated at Easter).

Aesthetic decline

Apart from some centres of excellence, the church has declined in its artistic commissioning (perhaps lacking funding, imagination, will or all three) and theatrical performances. Some of the major cathedrals have addressed this well; Chichester and Coventry in the post-war period, and many of the major cathedrals and some churches have instigated splendid modern commissions, often temporary and sometimes permanent (the font completed in 2008 by William Pye in Salisbury Cathedral deserves mention) but generally new commissions are few and weak. Their buildings remain of interest and are amongst the most visited of public buildings but these can be and are enjoyed independently of worship, as an historical curiosity. Perhaps that is their future. ✍✍

25 Attention

The school opposite the Square was built in 1882 and closed in 1976. The photograph below was taken in the summer of that year and shows Wyn Baker, the teacher who lived at no.33 and the children on the last day of the school's life.

Wyn was a popular head teacher of the school and lived in the village for over thirty years. She came from London, trained as a teacher and went to work in Zimbabwe with her sister, who married and settled there. Wyn returned to the UK in the early 1960s to care for her father and moved with him to Clifford Chambers, buying no.33 and doing the sort of extension and renovation work that was typical of that time. She was committed to the girl guide movement, running the Clifford Chambers Girl Guide Unit for many years and became District Commissioner. She retained her links with Africa, visited often and worked voluntarily for Amnesty International. She died in 1994 and her little house remained unsold for two years, as its poor construction and position down Duck Lane of one hundred paces over an uneven path, made it what estate agents call a 'character property'. It was found and bought by the Hosking Houses Trust in 1996 and largely rebuilt, while the several trees planted by Wyn were retained, pruned and cherished. ◎◎

Wyn Baker with her school children, 1976. Village archive

P The roperties

One of the oldest properties in the Square is no.35, owned by the Hosking Houses Trust. We acquired it in 1998 and our attitude to renovation of a property is to take things away, not install new material. We therefore removed partition walls and brick fireplaces, ceiling studding and door camouflage and found that, amongst other things, the front dormer window was original to the house. Once restored through many hours of rubbing with toothbrushes and caustic soda, its oak surround and panes of rolled glass with window frames of lead, iron, brass and copper were revealed.

We invited Nat Alcock to see this property and, good naturedly, he came and made an assessment of the late eighteenth century. We asked if he would write its history in the manner of the rectory and he sensibly said that there wasn't much to be said. So we asked if he would write the history of the whole Square and he agreed.

In our first chapter we distinguished between different sorts of history, and this is an illustration of such differentiation. Much of our subject matter throughout this book has depended on historical research but also on surmise and association. Dr Alcock's chapter on the properties proved to be the ultimate study of ownership and architecture and so detailed in historic, archival and architectural detail that some of his chapter had become significantly dissimilar to the others.

Therefore, the entire text of Dr Alcock's research is included on our website, with two similarly exact studies that he made previously of the rectory and no.19, further down the village. This material demonstrates his stature as an architectural and archival historian and the village is privileged to have attracted his professional attention. His prepared material as it is included here takes our study of the Square forward.

The houses in the Square

Nat Alcock

The Square is a group of sixteen close-set houses next to the church, which were formerly eighteen houses. Although one of the houses (no.24) was built in the sixteenth century (and possibly earlier) as was no.29 that has since been rebuilt and a further one (no.35) that dates from the late eighteenth century, most date to the early to mid-nineteenth century and were developed after 1804.

The four adjoining houses along the street (nos.20-23) are included in this survey because they formed part of the original properties in the same ownership as nos. 24-27.

The lane running beside nos.29-32 is known now as Duck Lane. The name is first documented in 1910 but may well have been coined when this part of the Square was developed into separate cottages in the 1830s.

The axis of the Square is orientated north-east, which is regarded as north in this chapter.

The gradual development of the houses around the Square can be followed principally from the lists of its inhabitants. For the western section, the main developments were the addition of nos.26 and 27, before 1824, and the replacement of a single cottage by the terrace of four houses, nos.20–23, in about 1865. The eastern section is more complicated, since two buildings (nos.29 and 35) appear to have predated the main house, no.28. From 1727 until 1806, only a house and a smithy are mentioned, which can be identified with nos.35 and 29 respectively. Following the building of the main house (no.28), it seems that a new blacksmith's shop was built (no.36/7), and by 1838 the range behind no.28 had become four cottages. With the cessation of its use by blacksmiths, between 1853 and 1861, the forge became two cottages and the final cottages (nos. 33 and 34) were added at the rear. ◎◎

nos. 20, 21, 22, 23

nos. 24/25, 26, 27

no. 28

nos. 29, 30, 31, 32

Plan of the Square,
house numbers 20 – 37
(once eighteen houses, now
sixteen), their enclosed gardens,
Duck Lane and unclaimed land, the
church and churchyard, the rectory,
the River Stour and its flood lines.
The Western section includes nos. 20-27
and the eastern section nos. 35-37

Contains Ordnance Survey data
© Crown copyright and database right 2013

no. 33

nos. 35, 36/37

69

The Morris Farm

A farmhouse that belonged to the Morris family from 1649-1801, this house (no.24) was divided into two cottages by 1800. While visual assessment dates it from around 1600, scientific dating suggests that it may be a century earlier; further tests are being done to verify this but whether or not these are conclusive, it remains the oldest building now surviving in the Square. It is now of two bays, with a modern lean-to range at the rear that may well replace an earlier structure, and it may also have had a further bay at the south end, though the southern gable, which is now of brick, retains no evidence for this. The plan of the upstairs rooms is the same as the ground floor, except that bay I was partitioned into two at a comparatively early date; bay II is also partitioned, but more recently.

The structure is of timber framing in square panels, three squares high and with four panels in each bay, although the extensive alterations obscure the original arrangement and the rear framing is mostly concealed. The framing is somewhat erratic, suggesting difficulties with the available timber.

As the house now exists, it lacks either an early fireplace or a clear original staircase position. If indeed it had a further room at the south end, this could have contained both of these. The expected inglenook fireplace might also have been in the south half of bay II, where the joists have been replaced; it would have been replaced by the present corner fireplace, which must be of the same date as the brick south gable wall.

Two probate inventories survive for the Morris farm: those of George Morris, 1719 and Robert Morris, 1737. The first gives good details of his household goods, in seven rooms: parlour, hall, pantry, day house [dairy], brewhouse, kitchen, over the hall. This suggests a house with three main rooms, parlour, hall and kitchen, consistent with it having originally had an additional room at the south end. The subsidiary rooms were perhaps in a rear lean-to, as suggested above. One upstairs room alone is named, probably not because this was the only one existing but because the others were empty or whatever they contained did not belong to him. At the time of his death, George Morris seems to have been living on his own, since his wife had died and his son was living in Stratford.

Robert Morris's inventory is minimal, simply listing 'goods' in three rooms, the best chamber, the little room and the middle room. Although we cannot be certain, the absence of either a hall or a kitchen strongly suggests that these were simply a set of upstairs rooms, rather than a complete house. He may well have handed over the house to his son, before his death in September 1737.

Nos.26 and 27

These two brick-built cottages each had one main room, apparently with rear lean-tos; the windows have single-brick segmental-arch heads. They have undergone recent extensive internal modernisation and contain no visible dateable features. From the documentary evidence, they must have been built between 1804 when William Buller acquired the western side of the Square, as a messuage and cottage, and 1828 when he bequeathed six cottages.

Nos.20–23

This row of four identical cottages is built as two mirror-image pairs. It uses brick in Flemish bond, with varied colour shades, but the bricks are not very well selected, giving a rather mottled appearance, while the segmental window arches use headers rather than alternating headers and stretchers (as at no.28). The rear walls have courses of Flemish bond separated by one to three courses of stretchers.

Each house comprises a main room, divided at the rear from the staircase and a small room interpreted as a pantry. Behind these, the rear room, which must have been the kitchen, has a chimney and fireplace, adjoining that of the next house. The upper floor provides a large room in the main block and a room over the kitchen (now used as a bathroom, but presumably originally a bedroom). The space over the pantry contains the stair to the attic, which is lit by a rear dormer. The roof is carried on chamfered purlins (probably reused) spanning between the brick partition walls. In 1910, the cottages were described as having three bedrooms with a kitchen (the main room), back kitchen and pantry. Privies stood in the yard behind the terrace, and they also had pigsties.

Internally, in no.22 (the only one examined for the purpose of this report), few features are visible, but a number of original vertical-boarded doors survive and the main upstairs room retains its fire grate. This is a simple Pantheon-pattern bedroom hob-grate, probably made by the Coalbrookdale Company near Ironbridge, Shropshire, ostensibly dating from circa 1830–45. However, the documentary evidence, in particular the will of William Buller in 1864 compared to the 1871 census, shows an increase from six to eight cottages between 1864 and 1871. Thus, this row of four cottages must have replaced the cottage divided into two, probably soon after it was bought in 1864 by Henry Baker, a builder. The fire grate may well have been among Henry Baker's old stock when the cottages were built (although they may also have continued in production for longer than suggested), or it may have been reused from the old cottage.

No. 28

This very neat house at the north end of the Square appears rather tall and narrow. However, this arises mainly from that fact that it was raised from two to three storeys soon after being built. The original front elevation is in Flemish bond (alternating headers and stretchers in each course), with pale headers and rather darker stretchers giving a chequered effect (a late example of classic Georgian brickwork). The alternating brick colours in the segmental window arches are particularly notable. The side elevation is much less well built, almost entirely in stretchers, with Flemish bond for every fourth or fifth course. The raised upper storey has the same style, but the bricks are slightly lighter than those below, giving it a paler appearance. The raising is particularly clear on the gable, where the original chimney is flanked by the later brickwork.

The house has only two rooms in plan, with a stone-flagged cellar under the eastern one. These probably served as kitchen (west) and parlour (east), the latter's boarded rather than solid floor reflecting its superior status. Both ground-floor rooms have axial ceiling beams, but they are incompletely chamfered and were probably originally plastered. The cellar had a stone-flagged floor (now replaced), and a raised stone stand for barrels or bowls (a thrall). Its transverse ceiling beam is chamfered but unstopped, and holds a number of heavy nails, probably used for hanging bacon or the like. An external access below the front window would have allowed heavy items to reach the cellar, perhaps including barrels, when the house was used as a pub. The house may well have been associated with a detached single-storey rear kitchen, standing to its north-west. This would have been reached through the door in the back kitchen wall, and the pump for the house stands in the former yard beyond this. This room was later used as a shoemaker's workshop.

The narrow staircase is placed between the two rooms. Unusually, it does not have a passage beside it, which caused a problem when the house was raised since it did not allow for another flight of stairs to be inserted above it. Thus, the attic is reached by a stair running along the rear wall of the house, behind the eastern room. This room contains the most notable original feature of the house: the fire grate. This has been identified as a fine late eighteenth-century Bath-pattern hob-grate with classical decoration, either made by the Coalbrookdale Company or the Carron Company of Falkirk, Scotland. Remarkably, it retains its wrought-iron chimney-crane for supporting a pot or kettle over the fire, although it is not clear why this would have been needed in a first-floor bedroom.

In 1880, the house was described as: 'All that substantial and well-built freehold licensed beer-house, containing: tap room, smoke room, parlour, four bedrooms, kitchen, back kitchen, two pantries, brewhouse and outbuildings, with large productive garden well-planted with choice fruit trees'. How all these rooms fitted into the house is not entirely clear. Was the tap room (where beer was presumably drawn from barrels into jugs, etc.) perhaps in the cellar? The kitchen, back kitchen, pantries and brewhouse must certainly have been in the back buildings.

The dating of the grate to 1780–98 suggests that the house might have been built before the sale to John Garfield in 1806; however, it is much more likely that Garfield undertook the building, with the help of the large mortgage he raised at the time of his purchase, rather than that it was built by the changing and absentee previous owners. The documentary evidence also suggests that the house did not exist in 1806. The addition of the upper floor cannot be closely dated, but may have taken place after Elizabeth Garfield married John Rouse in 1824, to provide more space for their family.

Nos. 29–32 Duck Lane

The first pair of these houses has been completely rebuilt on approximately its original footprint, and now provides no useful historical evidence. However, two of Rev Pippett's photographs show them in 1901, giving important information about the development of the Square. Nos. 29 and 30 were timber-framed, and

the only thatched building in the Square. They used square-panel framing, apparently of two bays. The pair must date to the early seventeenth century, and can perhaps be identified as the blacksmith's forge before the building of no.28 cut it off from the open part of the Square. Nos.31 and 32 are of brick and slate, a pair of mirror-image cottages with a central chimney, probably originally with one main downstairs room and larger and smaller bedrooms upstairs. The documentary evidence suggests that they were built somewhat before 1838.

Nos.35 and 36/7

These buildings form a single range on the east side of the Square, and are both brick built. No.35 appears to be the oldest building on the eastern side of The Square, although we have little direct dating evidence; the interior of no.36/7 has not been examined. The step in the brickwork at the rear, and the straight joint on the front show that they were built separately, with no.35 the earlier, using small and irregular bricks, in contrast to the larger more regular ones (machine-made?) of nos.36/7. No.35 uses alternate courses of Flemish and stretcher bond, and no.36/7 has courses of Flemish bond separated by three courses of stretchers. The most notable feature of no. 6/7 is the long timber lintel on the front elevation, identifying a former wide opening and indicating that this was originally not domestic, with the tall chimneys being added when it was converted to cottages.

No.35 contains a very irregular chamfered ceiling beam that appears to be of beech, while the elm joists are more neatly chamfered with run-out stops. The purlins are also of elm. Although these features are not closely dateable, they are consistent with the later eighteenth century, and the use of chamfered joists strongly indicates that this was a domestic building. It probably had a fireplace against the northern gable.

The details are consistent with the interpretation suggested above: that no.35 was the original blacksmith's house, while no.36/7 was his shop, probably constructed shortly after 1806 when no. 28 was built as a new house for John Garfield, and the earliest part of the complex, no.29, was no longer useable as the shop.

Nos.33 and 34 Duck Lane

The last pair of cottages was added to the eastern section of the Square between 1853 and about 1861; no.34 has been rebuilt on its original footprint, so this description is of no.33. It is brick-built, less substantial than any of the other houses in the Square, using stretcher bond throughout in walls that are only one brick thick (4½ in). It and no.34 probably originated as similar blind-back cottages (with no windows in their rear walls), with one ground-floor room and two small upstairs rooms. They appear to have originally had the same plan. No.33 comprises a main room with fireplace and range, floored in large stone flags. The second, northern room is much narrower and probably served as a pantry, as well as giving access to the staircase at the back. Its floor is mostly of brick-sized lias slabs, set on edge, accompanied by one very large flat slab. ◎◎

The Square's inhabitants

Our information on the people who lived in the Square comes primarily from the censuses between 1841 and 1911. Later than this, the only source giving the names of villagers is the electoral registers, but these do not include street numbers, so it is impossible to identify individual residents. A few earlier names are known, but we have little information about them.

Some one hundred distinct names of the heads of the families occupying the eighteen houses of the Square have been found up to 1911. Sixty family surnames are found altogether, the majority (forty) with only one family living in the Square, but ranging up to a maximum of eight distinct families. The total number of people in the Square was fifty-six in 1861, and rose with the increasing number of houses to seventy-nine in 1891 before falling to sixty in 1901. The average household size was 3.5 in 1861, rising to 4.4 in 1891 and then decreasing to 3.3 in 1911.

By far the most common single occupation was that of 'agricultural' or 'farm' labourer, occasionally described more specifically as shepherds and stockmen or, like William Cockbill in 1901, as 'labourer with threshing machine' (though he was just a farm labourer in 1911). The grooms and gardeners were a step up from the labourers, presumably working mainly at the manor, though some of the bigger farms may also have had grooms. Relatively few of the inhabitants had more skilled occupations, apart from those living in no. 28 (see below). Several were sawyers or carpenters, including Thomas Watkins (1861, 1871), though in 1881 he was described as 'hedge carpenter', someone who specifically repaired fences. The Square also housed millers, bakers and carters, and a few people for whom literacy was necessary: the railway clerk, the church clerk and the road surveyors. Very few women who headed households were described other than as widows, but one was a laundress and one a charwoman. Selected inhabitants of the Square are discussed below, starting with those living in the 'big house', no. 28.

The occupants of no.28

This was the only house that was regularly occupied by its owners, starting with John Garfield, the blacksmith. He was not from Clifford Chambers, and is first identified there in 1779 on the occasion of his marriage to Ann Smith, widow. Her first husband was almost certainly Michael Smith, blacksmith, who had died in March of that year, leaving her with two small children, Michael and Marcella, and it seems plausible that John Garfield had come to the village as Michael's apprentice. Ann can probably be identified as Ann Morgan of Barford who married Michael Smith there on 2 October 1774. Their son Michael himself became a blacksmith in Clifford, as did his son Seth, both of them working at their smithy at no.53 Clifford on the south of the street.

John Garfield was succeeded in his craft by his son-in-law John Rouse and indeed the latter's widow, Elizabeth, who was herself described as 'blacksmith' in the 1841 census, taken immediately after her husband's death. John Rouse was not born in the village and it is plausible that he came to live there as an apprentice.

John and Elizabeth had two children, John (1825–51) and William (1838–51), who according to their father's will were to share his property between them on their mother's death in 1845, though John eventually inherited it all after his younger brother's death at the age of twelve. In 1851, John described himself as a 'smith master, employing one man', who was presumably the Joseph Rouse, possibly a cousin aged twenty-four and born in Marton, whom the census records as living in no.28 with John, his wife Avis, John's brother William and Avis's mother, Elizabeth Spiers.

With the deaths of both John and William Rouse in 1851, and Avis's marriage to William Mountain Fisher, the blacksmith's craft, which had been practised here since at least 1727, disappeared. For a while, until 1867 the house was just a residence, lived in by Avis and William Fisher. He was a Stratford grocer born in 1829, and in 1851 was working as a 'grocer's assistant' in Pangbourne, Buckinghamshire.

Perhaps William moved out briefly in 1867, the year he died, since on 15 January 1867 he leased the house to John Spilsbury, licensed victualler. By the next census in 1871, William's two orphaned children, William and Elizabeth, were respectively apprenticed to a farm bailiff in Quinton and at a boarding school called Lavington House in Stratford. No. 28 was occupied by John Spilsbury, aged 41, beer-house keeper, and his wife Lucy. No name is recorded for this pub, so it was probably known only as 'Spilsburys'. His family had lived in Clifford since at least 1780. Indeed one of them (probably Richard) was tenant of the eastern part of the Square sometime before 1806; he may well have been a wheelwright, like his son Thomas and grandson William. This Thomas Spilsbury, who had been born in 1780, was John's father. The 1841 and 1851 censuses show John still living with his parent(s), but by 1861, he was lodging with his brother William, and working as an agricultural labourer. It is clear that his innkeeping at no. 28 did not prosper, since by 1881 he was back as a lodger, this time with Thomas Holtom, elsewhere in the village; his wife had died in 1878.

In 1879 the house was leased (by Revd Francis Annesley and Benjamin Wyatt, presumably trustees for the Fisher children) to William Horton, described as 'whitesmith and bellhanger', and in 1881 as 'whitesmith and innkeeper' when he was living there with his wife Louisa and two daughters. It seems that he also did not find innkeeping profitable, since by 1891 he had gone back to Stratford, where he had been working in 1871 with his father, Charles, also a whitesmith; he and his father were living in adjoining houses in Rother Street.

After its ten or fifteen years as a beer-house, the house at the end of the Square was taken over by William Coldicott, whose family lived there for more than sixty years. He was a shoemaker, born in Welford-on-Avon, and by 1891 he and his wife Ann (herself described as a bootmaker in 1901) had a very large family: George, sixteen, also a shoemaker, Frank, fifteen, a carpenter, and five daughters, Leah, Rose Ann, Ada, Margaret and Eva, ranging in age from one to thirteen. In 1901 William and Ann were living with their son Frank, who by now had also become a shoemaker, and the three youngest children. By 1911 Frank was married and was living elsewhere in the village with his wife, Sarah Amelia, and their two children. Later, presumably after William died in 1919, he moved to no. 28 where he was still living when the Clifford Chambers estate was sold in 1951. Indeed, it was his son, Ernest Frank Coldicott, who then bought the house (for £575); Ernest died in 1982.

Other families

Eight or nine individuals named Rouse headed households in the Square, including Avis and John, but they were not all members of the same family and were only distantly connected to each other (if at all). Thus, George Rouse, living in no.31 from 1881 to 1901, came from Welford-on-Avon. John, in no.37 in 1881, was born in Atherstone-on-Stour; a tragedy seems to be hinted at in his family, since from 1891 to 1911 the house was occupied by his wife Jane alone and John is nowhere to be seen; in 1901 Jane was working as a charwoman. The romantically named Egbert Rouse, (his sisters were called Minna, Florence and Livinia), was a groom/gardener, no doubt working at the manor. He was born in Blockley in 1869 and lived at no.26 in 1901 and 1911, and no doubt later; he was buried in the Clifford churchyard in 1940, and his wife of many years, Rose Mezzellee (Beechey), also from Blockley, was still at no.26 in 1951; they had married in 1889 and she died in 1960.

Two related families called Salmon lived in the Square in the years around 1900: Thomas and Mary Ann in no.23 and William and Margaret in no.21. Thomas, a shepherd in 1891, was born in 1833/4, the son of Thomas senior and Sophia Salmon. His elder brother, George, himself living in no.26 the Square in 1861, was the father of William, a journeyman miller, probably working for R.S. Smith at Clifford Mill. However, the family was not one that had been long established in Clifford; Thomas senior was born in Preston-on-Stour and perhaps moved to Clifford in the 1820s.

The Charlot family was not particularly extensive in the Square, but had been established in Clifford Chambers since the later eighteenth century, and the intriguing name suggests just possibly that they came originally from France; there are several variations of the name in the records. The first recorded members are Richard and Ann Charlot, who had their first child, William, in 1786, with eleven more baptised up to 1813. An Ann Charlot was buried in 1798, suggesting that Richard had married again, with his second wife also Ann. Their son John, with his wife Mary and son Edward, were living at no.24 the Square in 1841, but had moved elsewhere in the village by 1851; John and Mary died, respectively, in 1869 and 1867. The only other Square resident was Benjamin Charlot, the son of John's brother William. In both 1841 and 1851, he and his wife Sarah were living with his father-in-law Richard Field, though not in the Square; in 1851 they had five children living with them. By 1861 he had moved into the Buller cottage, with son Frederick only, though Charlotte Wa(r)ters and her three children were boarding with him; his middle son, Richard, was working as a servant at Clifford Hill Farm. It is not clear when Benjamin died, or what became of his wife Sarah.

One other member of the Charlot family is recorded in Clifford in the 1830s. This is Richard, one of William and John's brothers, with his wife Elizabeth. Regrettably, it was reported to the Gloucestershire Quarter Sessions in November 1830 and October 1832 that he had deserted his wife, leaving her chargeable to the parish. On both occasions he was sentenced to a month's hard labour in the House of Correction at North Leach. However, we must be very doubtful that he actually appeared to serve his term. He seems not to have returned to the village and cannot be identified confidently in the 1841 census.

Richard Garfield Beesley is recorded in no.33 the Square in 1891, though he was born in Clifford and had been living elsewhere in the village with his family since 1851. His name intrigues, suggesting a connection with John Garfield, the blacksmith; and indeed researching the link has revealed what must have been a village scandal in its day. He was baptised on 5 December 1819, son of Alice Beesley but with no father named, and the same is true for his sister Caroline (1817) and brothers William and Joseph (who died within a few weeks). Alice Beesley married William Randell in 1831 and had four more children (though three of them died) before her own death in 1836.

Bearing in mind the Garfield family connection, Alice can be identified as John Garfield's granddaughter. Her mother was his daughter, also Alice, who married Robert Beesley in Birmingham in 1802, and the younger Alice was christened in Clifford in 1804; Robert probably died in 1807, when a person of this name was buried at Clifford. The elder Alice had moved to Wolvercote, Oxfordshire by 1809, when she married Richard Field, a blacksmith (not the same Richard who lived in Clifford). They had three children baptised there, John, George and Caroline, but by 1841 (and probably long before then) she was back in Clifford. She features in John Garfield's will, written in 1825 in which he left £3 to his daughter Alice Field. In the 1841 census, she was the head of a household (presumably a widow, as is recorded in 1851), living with her son George Field, Hannah Randell, her nine-year-old orphaned granddaughter, and also a Richard Field, the right age to be Richard Garfield Beesley (who is not identifiable anywhere else in the census), who would also have been her grandchild. It seems entirely possible, therefore, that her daughter Alice was rather a wild child, who had four illegitimate children with an unknown man before settling down with William Randell and going on to have four more children of whom only Hannah survived infancy.

Richard Garfield Beesley married Mary Tracy in 1842; she was the daughter of Henry and Ann Trac(e)y (a laundress in 1851), who were living in the Buller cottage in the Square in 1841. They had a son, George, in 1843, but Mary died in 1847 and Richard married a second wife, Alice Field, another Clifford girl and the daughter of Richard and Elizabeth Field.

Richard Beesley was an agricultural labourer in 1841 and 1851, but by 1861 had become a carter, and in 1871 and 1881 he and his large family were living at Sheep Leys Farm, where he was farm bailiff for Revd Annesley. In 1891, at the age of 71, he had retired and was living with Alice at no. 33, perhaps until he died in 1898, when she moved into the Rectory Cottages with her daughter and son-in-law, Fanny and John Betteridge. Alice died in 1903.

Identified occupancy 1901

Two of Revd Pippett's photographs of the Square in about 1901 show some of the occupants standing outside their cottages, and indeed it is possible to suggest names for several people in the most informative one. In the foreground, outside the door of no.24, the two women must be Elizabeth, the wife of Frederick Mullis, and their daughter, another Elizabeth, who was aged 12 in 1901. The small boy beside them is less certain, but is perhaps the younger Rouse boy from no.26, Nelson, or perhaps Egbert (respectively five and eleven years old in 1901). Standing in the doorway of no.26 behind must be Rose Rouse, their mother. Indeed,

in the lower photograph, a man is just visible in the doorway, who must be her husband, the elder Egbert. The young-looking man at the back is presumably Frank Coldicott, rather than his father William, and the boy to the right may be the elder of the two Rouse boys.

The bottom photograph also shows a young girl to the right of the Square, who might well be either Clarrie or Minnie Rouse, eight or nine years old in 1901. It is notable in both the photographs how well-dressed everyone was; clearly they were in their Sunday best, and the photographs were taken in the late morning, with the sun falling almost from the south. ◉◉

Two photographs of people in the Square in 1901

The Church House and Village school

One building in the Square belonged to the parish. It stood at the southern end, in the corner of the churchyard, and it can be seen on the 1880 sale plan and also on the first edition 1:2,500 Ordnance Survey map (1887, surveyed 1883), although it had disappeared by the time of the second edition in 1905, just before it might have appeared in one of the early photographs of the village.

This building was the village school, in use until 1883. Its history at this period can be discovered from two sources: the Vestry Minute Book (1873–1914) and the School Logbook (1877–1904). The logbook reveals the desperate problems that the school faced. For example on 24 July 1882, sixty-six children present in the morning and seventy-two in the afternoon, but they had desk room only for thirty: 'the school room is so much crowded it is impossible to keep good order'. The annual government reports (as recorded in the logbook) were increasingly damning about the 'poorness of the buildings and the crowded state of the school room'. At a vestry meeting in January 1882, it was agreed to take steps to procure a site for a new school for the parish, and in March it was agreed that the school would be built as soon as possible, with the owners of land contributing to the expense, and 'the tenants will do all the hauling'; James West of Alscot Park, the lord of the manor, presented the site, and the total cost was £766. On 19 March 1883, 'Removed to the New School' is triumphantly recorded. The new village school survived until 1976, when a brief history of it was written for the parish magazine by its last teacher, Winifred Baker.

As soon as the school had moved, a vestry meeting decided that the old school room should become a Reading Room for the men of the parish during the winter months, and set up a committee to arrange it. However, in June 1885 it was agreed instead that the old school building would be taken down and the churchyard wall built up.

What disappeared as the result of this decision was a building with a much longer history than just its use as the schoolhouse. The most significant information about it comes from an inquiry in 1685 undertaken by the Commissioners for Charitable Uses (predecessors of the Charity Commission), who investigated disputes about charitable property and bequests. It had been claimed that a house called the Church House in or near the churchyard in Clifford Chambers should belong to the inhabitants, but the rents were being taken by Henry Dighton, lord of the manor. Among the witnesses was William Cale, aged 70 or more, who said that the house was mostly in the churchyard with a little part of the corner in the adjoining ditch; the upper room was a school house and the rest a meeting place. Frances Morris, widow, aged 70 (who lived across the yard at the Morris farmhouse), remembered that the old house, very decayed, had been rebuilt by the inhabitants. Philip Cale, 76, declared that the parishioners usually met there on the Monday, Tuesday and Wednesday of Whitsun week.

Plan of the Square showing the Church House in the corner of the churchyard. Sale plan, 1880

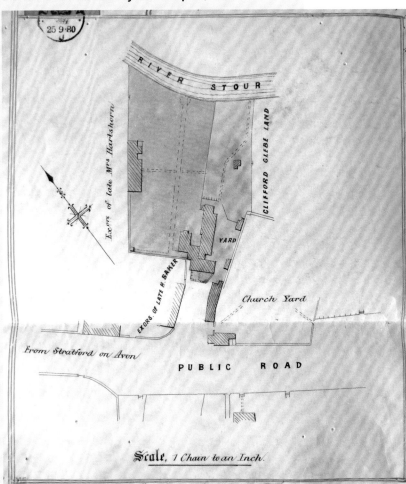

Abraham Swan of Ilmington was in 1656 the schoolmaster there, and taught school in the upper room, while one Hancock and his wife, and (Edward) Clark and his wife, dwelt in the lower room. Edward also gave evidence, and said that Hancock was his father-in-law and that he had also taken care of a bastard child for the parish (who would have had the responsibility for his/her upkeep in the absence of anyone else). Most importantly, he said that it was Job Dighton who had given him permission to live there, implying that the house belonged to the manor.

The result of the court case is not known, but the evidence strongly suggests that it was indeed a parish house. Typically, in the medieval period these houses would have been used for parish meetings and feasts (perhaps on St Helen's Day, 21 May). Later it became the village school, perhaps particularly after Thomas Jackson's Charity provided a regular income to pay a schoolmaster. It is clear, also, that it was regularly found useful for accommodating poor families for whom thereafter there appears to have been no ready accommodation. ☙

Full text with references and further illustrations are on www.hoskinghouses.co.uk under *Round the Square and Up the Tower*: 'The Properties' by Dr. Nat Alcock

The People

On our opening page we dedicated this book to 'the people and their creatures' of the Square. We intend this word to refer not only to the animals, domestic and feral who have lived here but also to unborn or new-born babies who died.

In the south east corner of the churchyard beside its front wall is the place where the very young were buried in marked or unmarked graves. Recently, a family member arrived to find the grave of his childhood brother and installed a stone to John Bentley who had died aged eight in 1941. Often, unbaptised children and unborn miscarried 'creatures' were buried in the dark, north side of the churchyard along with the suicides and the unclaimed vagrants. Our sunny corner is a better resting place. We are now considering further the lives of the people who have lived in the Square, on this hump of land that is just high enough to avoid the river's flood water. Information comes from several sources of which the main ones are:

Parish registers

Tombstones and memorials

Paper data

Oral and anecdotal data

Medieval church chest

Parish registers

Research by Val Horsler

In a far-sighted and controlling administrative measure of 1538, Thomas Cromwell, Henry VIII's first minister, decreed that every parish must keep a register of baptisms, marriages and burials. During the reign of Elizabeth it was further decreed that the registers should be entered on parchment (made from hides and therefore more durable) and that earlier paper copies should be transcribed. They were to be kept in a locked chest and, from 1597, a second copy had to be made and sent to the bishop. In 1812 new legislation required births, marriages and deaths to be entered in separate books specially printed for the purpose. Civil registration was introduced in 1837.

The Clifford Chambers registers between 1538 and 1812 are in three volumes, now in Warwick County Record Office. The earliest volume, in accordance with the Elizabethan decree, is on parchment; it was rebound at the end of the nineteenth century. The transcription of the registers in 1893 by Revd J. Harvey Bloom is kept in the archives of the Shakespeare Birthplace Trust. Of the original registers, volume I covers 1538-1740, volume II 1741-53 and volume III 1753-1812. There is only one recorded name of a registrar, and he seems to have wanted to make quite sure that readers of the register would know who he was: 'Thomas Urin his booke 1660

Thomas Urin is the keeper of this booke in this present yeare 1660 Thomas Urin Clarke of this parish'. Although there are breaks in the record between 1568 and 1575 and again from 1630-36, Clifford's parish clerks appear to have carried out their important task conscientiously and, as far as we can judge, competently.

The first volume is headed 'The Regester booke of Christenges Weddynges and buryalls done in the parish of Clifford Chambers in comitatu Gloucs as followeth annubus 1538'. The registrars were clearly literate, but they wrote down what they heard, hence the variety in the spelling of names, plus the bearers of the names would not often have an established spelling of them themselves. The first four baptisms recorded at Clifford in 1538 were those of 'Edw s of Jarra Cooke' on November 6, Joyce d of Jno Brown' on February 23, 'Elnor d Jno Mallarye' on 6 March and 'Jarram s Geo Hunt' on 24 March.

There were seven baptisms in 1539, five in each of 1540 and 1541 and then a mini-boom of eleven in 1542. Some years record only a single baptism, and other entries state 'born & bapt' on the same day, for a sickly baby who had to be received quickly into the church. The registrar sometimes added his own take. On 4 October 1547 there is an entry for the baptism of 'Marye borne of a stranger whose name is unknown', and in 1580, 'Mychaell son to Elizabeth Webb per Henry James so she sayth'.

Clifford seems to have stayed more or less the same size throughout the centuries covered by the registers, if numbers of baptisms are any guide; there were rarely more than ten a year, and usually around five or six. Numbers of burials in a year were at about the same level, and there were rarely more than one or two weddings a year between 1538 and 1753 when the second volume ends. The first two recorded in 1538 are those of Will Cale and George Hand, but no mention of the names of their wives!

Tracing made by Revd Pippet of baptismal entry 1557

Matching up of baptism and burial records points poignantly both to the frequency of infant death and to the early orphaning of young children. Elnor, daughter of Humfrie Welshe, was born in 1560, but her father did not live to see her grow beyond the age of five; his burial took place in 1565. The loss of more than one child in the same year was common: on 29 June 1582 Ellen, daughter of S. Olypher, was buried, and on 18 November of the same year so was 'John her brother'. The perils of childbirth are highlighted by the frequent burial of mother and child together, like 'Margery Aston and John her son' on 13 December 1548. In 1565 there were four burials within three days; was this the plague, which struck Stratford and its environs viciously around that time? And it can be safely assumed that Henry Prickett, who was baptised on 11 October 1578 'whose parents are unknown' is the same as Henry Prykes 'whose parents were unknown' and who was buried just ten days later.

The Jerome Cooke whose son Edward was the first to have his baptism recorded in the new register in 1538 was the joint lord of the manor of Clifford, until it was sold to Charles Rainsford in 1562. The frequent appearance of Charles's name in both baptismal and burial records as his sons and daughters were born and died indicates all too clearly how uncertain and short newborn life could be, regardless of the prosperity, and therefore higher standard of living, of the parents. His first four children appear to have survived the rigours of infancy, but the fifth, Margaret, died the year after her birth and of the following eight children only two certainly made it to adulthood, and the family lost both baby Edward and two-year-old Dorothea in the same month in 1553. Charles's wife Jane must have spent almost her entire married life pregnant; unsurprisingly, she predeceased her husband. His second wife, Frances, had no children and survived him.

These brief extracts show how tenuous life was for everyone and especially for poor children like 'Henry Prykes'. They would all have been buried in the churchyard somewhere, but memorials were only for those who could afford it. ◎◎

Tombstones and memorials

Survey by Daphne Bramwell 1980
Edited by Val Horsler

(Since this survey was made in 1980, some of the stones mentioned have become indecipherable.)

Daphne Bramwell was living in the village when she made a survey of the gravestones and monumental inscriptions prior to 1900 both within the church and in the graveyard, and matched them up, where she could, with the baptismal and marital records. It is a fascinating document, offering tantalising glimpses into the lives of Clifford's villagers: the duration of a long marriage, the sadness of losing a child, the relationships within families and between members of the community. They also indicate the longevity of some Clifford families, and show that in many ways St Helen's graveyard is a microcosm of this small community, at least how it was before the twentieth century made travel easier, split families up and made it necessary and possible for some long-standing members of the community to leave their ancestral village and for newcomers to take their place.

The unmarked mounds that used to be obvious in so many churchyards indicate the places of burial of the mass of people, such as those who lived in the Square. Gravestones and other monuments would have been erected only by the better off, and it is clear that the vast majority of burials in the graveyard are unmarked. Indeed, when the garden wall of no.35 collapsed a few years ago, the owner found bones tumbling into his garden: 'I tapped them back with a mallet and told them to lie quiet'. Nos.35 and 36/37 next door, the two houses on the eastern side of the Square, both have about a metre of earth banked up against their walls; graveyards tend to rise quite considerably in height over the centuries, evidence for the certain fact that burials would have taken place at St Helen's from the earliest days of the church's existence. Those walking today through the graveyard are stepping over the remains of villagers of Clifford going back to the very beginnings of occupation in this area.

There is no evidence for a charnel house here, such as there was at Holy Trinity in Stratford, for the bones of the long-dead, which had to be moved to make way for new burials. However, by 1955 the graveyard had become so full that there was no room for any more burials, and a piece of the rectory orchard was commandeered for the purpose. This is where most of the modern burials are sited.

None of the gravestones are earlier than the eighteenth century, probably due to the nature of the stone and the need to clear them away for new burials. The oldest stone legible when the survey was done is that of Henry Selvester (sic) who died on 16 June 1715 aged forty-one. As Daphne Bramwell says, it seems appropriate that the oldest extant gravestone should belong to this family because 'in 1266 Roger Silvester was one of the customary tenants of the manor and there are still (1980) Silvesters in the village'.

One of only a few gravestones of villagers who lived here in the eighteenth century, now almost illegible, commemorates John Rogers and his two wives.

He married the first, Ursula, in 1770 and had four children baptised in St Helen's. The year after her death in 1779, John married again. He and Mary had five children, of whom one died in infancy. Mary died in 1801 and John in 1808. There is a record of him receiving 14s 6d from the churchwardens in 1792 for winding the church clock.

Records and the gravestones of the Spiers family, yeoman farmers, indicate that they appear to have been a prominent force in the village from at least the early eighteenth century. Another local dynasty is that of the Salmons. Their forebear Thomas was not born or married in the parish, but by 1822 was working here as a labourer. He had at least six children, some of whom married and raised families in the village, and he himself rose to become bailiff of the Rectory Farm and, according to his gravestone, carried out his duties 'with exemplary honesty and fidelity for nearly forty years'. He died in 1875 aged seventy-seven, and his stone was erected by Arthur Annesley, brother of the rector, 'as a mark of esteem'. The name Salmon appears twice on the war memorial on the corner of the graveyard, one member of the family died in each of the world wars. John Salmon, who was killed in the Second World War, is remembered both on the memorial and on the Peace Bell hanging in the church belfry.

And there are also the Livelys (or Lifleys), parish clerks extraordinaires. John, the first on record at Clifford, was a labourer who married Hannah, daughter of a servant, at St Helen's in 1826; they are both buried in the graveyard. He became parish clerk and died in 1870, having held the office until the previous year. It then passed to his nephew William till his death in 1887, when his son John took over in his turn. He was parish clerk for an amazing sixty years until his death during the fearfully cold winter of 1947 in his eighty-eighth year. An article published in the summer of 1947, just after John's death, described his demeanour in church right up until the end: 'His dignified walk up the nave, his steady gait while mounting the steps of the chancel and the methodical way he turns to his desk and reaches for his spectacles all belie his years. In the truly traditional manner he leads the people, being first with the amens and responses, saying them in a loud voice.' The family tradition was to continue for a few years more in the person of John's son, John Henry, who held the office until 1952.

A large plot forms the family vault of the Annesleys: it is paved, surrounded by pink stone blocks and surmounted in the centre by a white marble cross on a three-stepped plinth. The inscriptions commemorate the Revd Francis Annesley, who died in 1882 aged eighty-two after thirty-four years as rector of Clifford, his nephew and son-in-law Francis Hanbury Annesley, who succeeded him as rector and died in 1904 aged seventy-seven, Francis Hanbury's wife (also his cousin) Maria, who survived him for less than a year, one of their children, Reginald, who died suddenly in 1882 aged seventeen and another son, Arthur Dighton Annesley, who was born in 1866 and died in 1943.

Many women, of course, were worn out by constant pregnancy and childbirth; it is noticeable that several

women buried in St Helen's graveyard died in their forties, just past childbearing age. But early death, by today's standards, was common in men too, several of whom in St Helen's graveyard were only in their thirties or forties when they died.

Others did manage to survive up to or beyond 'three score years and ten'. Thomas Harwood reached the grand age of eighty-eight before dying in 1848, and his wife Mary, who died two years before him, was seventy-seven. But even so their lives encompassed the sadness of early death: of their eight children baptised at Clifford, three died before reaching the age of six, two in the same year, and their daughter Sarah was only fifteen when she too died.

The large table tomb grave of a nine-month-old baby, Thomas Hayward, who died in 1859, was probably eventually intended for other members of his family too, but presumably proved too difficult to dismantle when the time came. His grandparents, Edmund and Jane Cockbill, who farmed at Clifford Hill, both died aged thirty-nine in 1843 and 1844 and are buried in Clifford, and it seems that the baby's mother, Elizabeth, inherited the farm and she and her husband lived and farmed there, producing five other sons who were baptised at St Helen's. But none of the rest of the family is buried here, and they presumably moved away, as in 1872 they were no longer farming at Clifford Hill.

A decorative headstone and slab are the grave markers of the Smith family. Richard Sidney Smith owned the forge mill and lived at Clifford Lodge. His first wife, with whom he had a large family, died aged forty-two and he then married the children's governess, who died aged forty-six, five years before her husband. Two of the children are also commemorated on the slab, and the small stained glass window next to the pulpit in the church was presented by the Revd Pippet in memory of Richard Sidney Smith, who was for many years the rector's warden.

This little window is evocative of the two small lancet windows in the porch of Holy Trinity church, Stratford, the first of which was placed there in 1870 by the vicar, John Day Collis, in memory of his wife, and the second, in 1879, in memory of Collis himself by his second wife, Elizabeth. She is buried in Clifford in the same grave as her first husband, Admiral Douglas Curry, who lived at

Shottery Hall, Stratford, where his widow continued to live after his death and during her second marriage. The grave in Clifford also remembers their daughter Mary Anne 'born 27 April died 16 May1848' and their son Douglas Edward, who was lost at sea in 1870.

Another accidental death remembered on a gravestone was that of William Garner, aged twenty-three, killed in 1872 'while signalling the railway trains between Warwick and Hatton'. He had been baptised in 1849, as was his brother Thomas, though their baptisms were on different dates nearly a month apart. They were presumably twins, and Thomas also died young, aged twenty-five, two years after his brother was killed on the railway. Indeed, the numbers of young deaths commemorated in this graveyard are truly shocking to modern perceptions. John Rouse was thirty-nine when he died and his wife Elizabeth made it to forty-eight; they left two sons, neither of whom survived them by very long. In April 1851, six years after his mother died, twelve-year-old William succumbed, to be followed in September of the same year by his older brother John, who was twenty-six. The verse on his grave reflects what must have been a deep need to take comfort in the hope of the hereafter:

Forgive blest shade the tributary tear
That mourns thy exit from a world like this
Forgive the wish that would have kept thee here
And stay'd thy progress to a seat of bliss

And finally to one of the most intriguing stones in the graveyard. A slightly raised table tomb west of the tower is the memorial of Susanna Lovel, 'queen of the gypsies'. The inscription reads 'In hopes of a joyful resurrection herein lieth the remains of Susanna Lovel who departed this life 5 July, 1812 aged seventy-two years. Major Lovel her husband erected this tomb in remembrance of a truly loving wife and affectionate mother.' For many years after her death passing gypsies would leave gifts of tobacco on her grave.

(Material on the memorials inside the church has been included in the chapter on the church.)

Of more modern memorials whether inside or outside there are none, although there are several tombs within the graveyard of villagers who have died in recent years; also, and there is also a cluster, by the east and south exterior walls of the chancel, of commemorative stones for villagers who have been cremated. Lavish memorials to the dead are mostly a thing of the past; their memory is more frequently kept alive today through charitable works or more practical objects. Moreover, funeral rituals have changed, with cremation often preferred to burial. It is notable at St Helen's that there are several instances of villagers who had lived elsewhere choosing to return to their childhood home to be buried, once again, a practice that has fallen into disuse with a more mobile and less firmly rooted populace. ◎◎

Full text for the church records, the graveyard and memorials survey are included on our website www.hoskinghouses.co.uk **under** *Round the Square and up the Tower* : 'The People'

Paper data

This book has already quoted and referred to a mass of paper data, as in our survey of parish registers and also in the chapter 'The Properties' where information from documentation is used extensively.

Therefore, we are using one example only, which is the photograph used by Nat Alcock of the people in the Square in 1901, and his identification of them (included in the last chapter). We are then making some surmises about their quality of life.

These people would be doing well if they kept food upon the table and raised their children without rickets. Their work was mainly on the land and with the manor, some casual work became jobs, such as groom and gardener and the women were laundresses and cleaners. They would probably all have laboured to bring in the harvest but they were socially a cut above the permanent farming gangs, which were especially hard for women, since they were unprotected when out in the fields from rough behaviour and rough weather.

In our 'A' section. we include 'Artisan artefacts' and these are hammers that show the trades that were carried on in and near the Square. There was also a midwife and a coffin-maker down the village, a cobbler, a carpenter and forge nearby. It took two world wars and the social upheavals they instigated, as well as the 1944 Education Act and the Welfare State to allow jobs to become trades and for the women to be able to stay at home. With the sale of properties in 1951 by the manor, those who lived in the Square took another step up the social ladder, becoming home owners. Under 'A for Acquisition', we discuss the prices, values and uses of houses in the Square over time, and acknowledge that today, owners are accomplished professionals servicing an affluent society often far away; computer consultants, airline pilots, the sports and entertainment industries are represented here because the Square has become a desirable place to live, for those who can afford today's prices.

Oral and anecdotal data

Research by Sally Abell

One good reason to knock nostalgia on the head is that the past, in all its vague vastness, was usually worse for women than for men, from the simple fact of bearing children. Recalling the 1880s, Flora Thompson writes of their village midwife, 'The old woman was not a certified midwife but she was a decent, intelligent old body, clean in her person and methods and very kind. For half a crown she came every morning for a fortnight to bath the baby and make the mother comfortable.' *Lark Rise to Candleford*.

These arrangements would probably have been much the same here, and a recent reminiscence from the Square from the 1940s (pre-welfare state) recalls: 'A capable midwife and female friends and relatives were on hand to clean up after the birth and mop down the rubber sheet that was brought in to protect the mattress.' Men were kept well out of the way but were summoned from the pub or the club when delivery was safely made; 'It's got a tail' shouted one happy (continued on page 82)

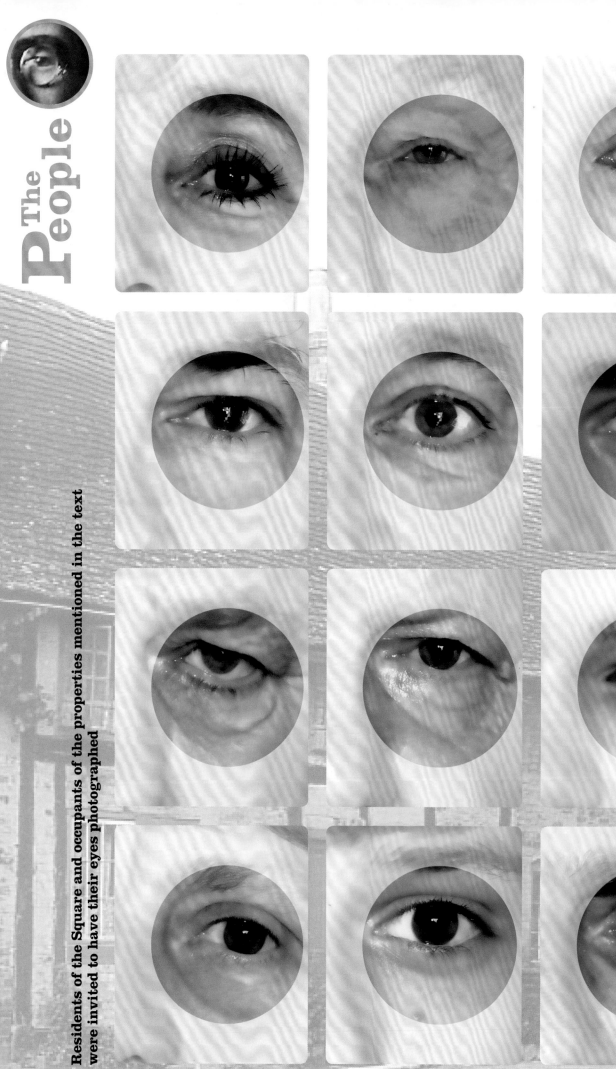

The People

Residents of the Square and occupants of the properties mentioned in the text were invited to have their eyes photographed

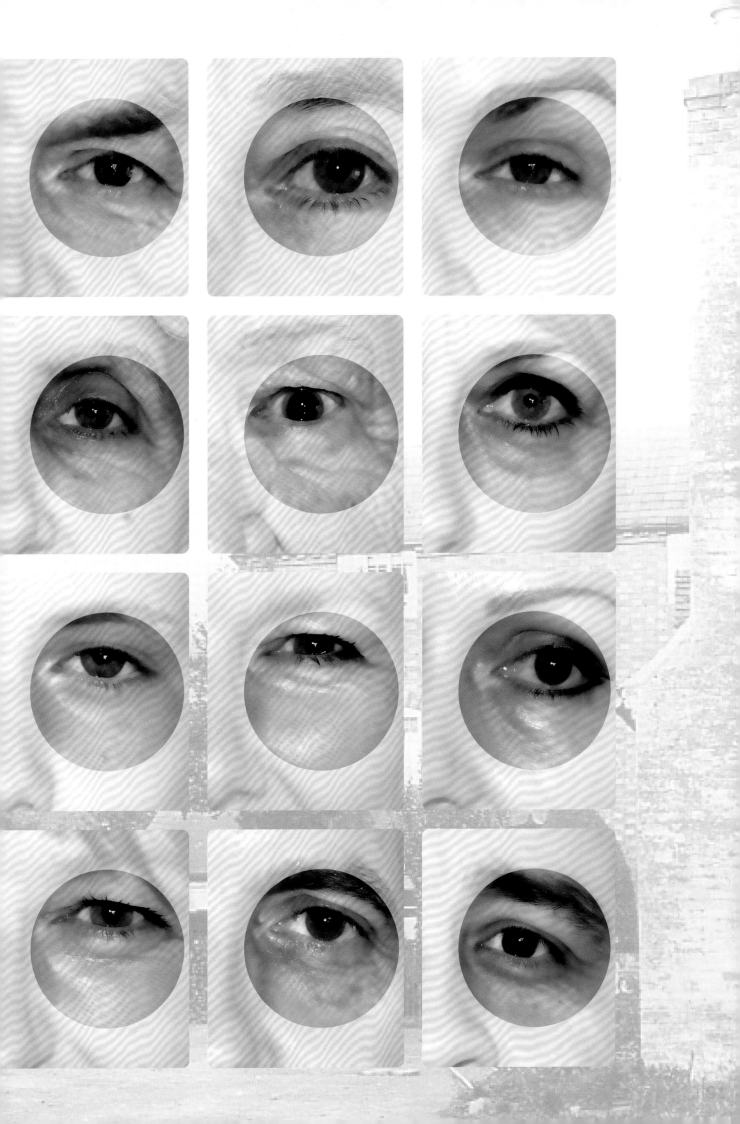

father (meaning he had a son) as he cycled around the village with the news. Deliveries were at home until the 1960s, and gas was used (from a portable cylinder) although if the mother had a cold, it was not administered and just depended on pulling on a knotted towel and counting the contractions ("each one was one less", one mother recalled).

In a skip in the Square in the 1990s when one of the houses was being cleared, a sanitary towel was found made from old curtain fabric, with the loops to tie to a waist belt and with a discoloured name tape. Such towels were all the protection women had available during menstruation, and they had to be hand-washed and dried and used again. The set of four night soil privies which are still there (now listed) and which served the houses in Duck Lane, were the only facilities for four families with women of child-bearing age and children; their use is still in living memory of one family (see below).

The mothers would have done their best, like most mothers, but would have had few resources. 'There was little room for their finer feelings in the mother's life. All her strength, invention and understanding were absorbed in caring for her children's bodies; their mental and spiritual qualities were outside her range'. *Lark Rise to Candelford.*

It would have been much the same here and until contraception arrived and was available (not freely available until the late 1960s), the old age pension in 1908, reliable anaesthetic in childbirth, short skirts and the bicycle, life for women was constrained. Then it changed radically with a host of solid incremental legislative achievements that mainly affected women: these included women's suffrage in 1928, the 1944 Education Act, the 1967 Abortion Act, the 1969 Family Law Reform Act, the 1975 Sex Discrimination Act besides changing attitudes to women's opportunities and domestic violence. Our grandmothers, let along those of previous generations, would regard such progress as wonderful, as indeed it is. Probably electricity and water made the most difference of all in daily life, when the most urgent task was cooking.

The grandmothers of those of us who are now ourselves old, recalled that during the winter there would have been oatmeal porridge and porridge and porridge again, and possibly a lump of fat bacon if you were lucky. Joseph Arch, who was the first agricultural labourer to become an MP in 1885, came from Barford, a village ten miles north-east of Clifford. He wrote of the labouring families' diet as burnt crust tea, skimmed milk and cheese. His mealtime grace was:

'O Heavenly Father bless us, and keep us all alive;
There are ten of us to dinner and food for only five.'

The poor (such as lived in the Square) would have had such a diet, with meal porridge and buttered roots, plus rabbits and birds as they were trapped. Within memory, fish caught in the river were a staple food, pike tasted a bit like cod, and there was chub and eel, which could be jellied. This is why feast days were so important because they offered more and different food; the landowner

may have paid starvation wages but would provide a fine harvest supper and give Christmas benefits.

An elderly former inhabitant of the Square recalls; "In the early years of the twentieth century no.24 was the village slaughterhouse. Pigs met their end here at the hands of Darkie Mullis. The deed took place in the outhouse shared with no.23 and the animal would then be returned to its owner for salting down and consumption in the winter months". Most people would have had a pig and hens, and grown vegetables; their gardens and land were units of production and if there was only one cooking pot on the fire, it did not mean there was only one thing to eat, but dumplings and meat would be carefully wrapped in cloths and cooked among the vegetables in the pot.

The greatest change to cooking was iron fireplaces and the iron range, which even our small houses would eventually have had in the late nineteenth and early twentieth centuries; (this is discussed in Nat Alcock's chapter). They were slow and needed dry fuel and constant attention, but they heated water, cooked the food, warmed the house and were more reliable than an open fire.

The Second World War galvanised food production and, to those of us who remember those days, no scrap of food should ever be wasted again. The classic routine of ration-time meal planning was for a family to have a joint of meat on Sunday, cold with salad Monday, mince on Tuesday, fritters (with the gristly bits put through the mincer) on Wednesday, omelettes on Thursday, fish on Friday and go to granny's house on Saturday. Then start again. A packed lunch was a hard-boiled egg, a bread and butter sandwich and an apple. It's a long way from a prawn salsa wrap.

Eating depends, then as now, on teeth. The teeth of even young people were often taken out and replaced with dentures just to save pain and trouble (this could even be a wedding present for a bride) but this depended on anaesthetic. The NHS included free dentistry in 1948, but even in Coronation photographs from 1953, older people are shown with the sunken cheeks of the toothless. In previous time, teeth (like all aspects of health) depended on luck. None of the people in Revd Pippet's photographs are smiling because they would have had bad teeth.

Gardens even up until the 1960s were kept under cultivation for food. Photographs of Clifford's street show few trees because they kept the sun off ripening fruit and a railing in front to fend off anything that might flatten the cabbages. The three-and-a-bit acres that belong to the united houses of the Square and including unclaimed land, could then as now feed its sixteen houses at a push.

Gardens are now big business and indicators of ownership and even of wealth and status. It has become an opportunity for expenditure and display and the plants available are almost as varied from across the globe as the food. Tree ferns and bags of peat, whose removal in quantity damage the environment from which they come, are available nearby. It takes a very determined effort on the part of some devout Green activist to make us think again.

It was originally the intention of this book to include several personal reminiscences from those who had at one time lived in the Square, some of whose family memories extended back to the sale of the properties by the manor in 1951. However, as our several contributors delivered their work and the book's final content became apparent in its entirety, these personal voices seemed too different in tone to the other accumulated material. We therefore decided to include them elsewhere in the text as appropriate and to use here just one, from the Wilks at no.32 whose three generations of wedding photographs we include under 'A for Affection'.

It is hard to imagine today just how labour-intensive the simplest acts of living were in the even recent past. When John and Maisie Wilks first settled into the chocolate-brown rooms of their cottage in 1956 there was no hot water, no bathroom and a well where the television is now. The wash-house was next door and, having pumped water from the well, a fire was lit beneath the copper and women gathered to do their washing. Sociable it may have been, convenient it was not. Even for those with the luxury of a Burco boiler, nearly every day was wash-day since the water took a good while to heat. Clothing and linen were then washed by hand and put through the ringer. Clothes lines ran from every house to the church wall opposite and flapping washing had to be ducked and dodged, except on Sundays when no-one hung the washing out. It was on the instructions of Mrs. Douty at the manor that children were not allowed to play outside on a Sunday.

As there was no mains water and no sewage system until the 1970s, calls of nature were conducted in one of the outdoor privies where the deposit bucket had to be emptied and its contents buried on a regular basis. There were, occasionally, consequences like the time when John and Maisie's toddler son Philip, together with his cousin Graham, decided to dig for treasure one summer's afternoon. They had not reached an age where disgust entered their thoughts and their 'foul' play was only discovered when they went home extremely dirty and smelly.

In our 'A for Accuracy' section, sanitation arrangements are shown.

The four closets are extant and neglected, even though they are Grade II listed. One still has seats inside; once there would have been wider seats with different sized holes for children: these seats would all have been distempered once a year and one former resident recalls that the scratchings on them came from the women's stocking suspenders. Toilet paper was newspaper torn into squares with a hole in the corner and hung from a string. Often, the doors and insides were painted pink or blue, for the men and the women.

During World War II, there were several evacuees who came to the village from Birmingham and these extra people put extra pressure on all facilities, food, schooling and use of these privies. One family was offered the then empty no.37. There were thirteen children and one exhausted mother in a two-up, two-down cottage. Their names have been lost as has that of the boy who came to no.34 and continued to visit until the 1980s, apparently remembering with affection his time in this pleasant, safe but then unsophisticated place. ◎◎

Prognosis

'The faulty connection between town imperatives and country living remains one of the great national issues of our time'.

Andrew Motion in a review of Craig Taylor's *Return to Arkenfield, Guardian* March 2006

As suggested in our Introduction, the village has in recent times attracted people who have superimposed their urban requirements on previous rural self-reliance with mixed results. We wish to end this book with some thoughts on this and what the future might hold.

Aerial view of the Square, the land, the river and the church
John Miller, *Chair to Air,* 1998

John Miller was a paraplegic who had a small plane adapted for his wheelchair. He died in 2012 and this is printed in his memory.

The opening of the television programme *The Vicar of Dibley* shows an aerial view of the archetypal village; fields, the church, the manor and the houses clustered around with no urban sprawl or nearby busy road. This is the sort of image used in posters during the last war ('This is what you are fighting for') and for hundreds of books and thousands of postcards ever since.

The aerial view above shows the small part of this village that has been the subject of this book; just over three acres with land and the river, the modern sixteen homes and the church. It looks enchanting but, from the air, it does not reveal many aspects of contemporary village life.

Since the 1960s, changing patterns of farming and village ownership have driven many people from their native places, eroding the fabric and feeling of rural life. In this village, it is the original local family, breeding animals for slaughter, burning the fowl feathers in the back yard, sluicing the blood down the drain who are now seen as the anachronism; but when a rabbit needs to be drawn or a chicken killed, this is the family with the necessary skills. If the cockerels escape from their rickety pens and fly up into the trees and call to each other from dawn as a surprisingly orderly choir, it is very difficult to stop them. Shoot them or put up with it are the alternatives.

Some of the research for this book has involved tracking local families, such as those commemorated with gravestones or memorials and also the humbler, uncommemorated people who lived in the Square, such as those named in Nat Alcock's chapter and who are recorded in the last chapter. In both cases, this family hierarchy of inheritance and habitation has, as in almost all villages, been largely broken because of family mobility, emigration and education and rocketing house prices.

With the loss of the old trades (the coffin-maker, the cobbler) so also has vanished those people who, because they were here every day, could undertake the responsibilities of the community. Digging ditches to relieve flood water, winding the church clock and ringing the bells, mending fences, retrieving lost boats and oars, dealing with foxes, laying out the dead, helping deliver babies, mediating between warring neighbours, all of them are duties that still need attention today, but now they tend to be done by paid outsiders. With the loss also of the post office, the shop, the school and the activities associated with the church (the choir, the bell ringers and the Sunday school) and with fun (the guides, the cricket team) the central objective of village life is diffused.

New people bring money and energy but they are often not able to lavish time and loyalty on a community that would benefit from such experience. But money and energy are valuable assets. The Pippet photographic archive from 1895 to 1906 shows properties in the Square that we would consider to be in a parlous state of disrepair. Broken gates, farmyard mess and wretched thatches were due to poor maintenance by the owners, who were the family in the manor, and there was resentment of this at the time. But it was also due to the occupants' lack of time and money when the urgent need was putting food on the table.

Nowadays, those same properties are extended, idealised and immaculate. Money has stopped them from falling down (except for no.34 which fell down before money could be spent on it) but too much money can mean that they are prettified without being enriched at a more fundamental level.

The urban dweller relies on others for food and life's other essential services. Being released from such basic labours, they can then do other things; this is the basis of urban society. This is the major change in the village, that it is no longer willing and is increasingly unable to support itself in food and services but uses the car to import those necessities and comforts, and earn the money to supply them. This has a dramatic effect in the way the village is regarded and used.

Nos 31 and 32 before 1905

Prognosis

The opening of the M40 in 1990 and the development of Birmingham Airport from its minuscule wartime usage, mean we can all go anywhere, anytime. That is what those who live in the Square today are able to do in pursuit of the income to create their rural dream. Wonderful, and such a contrast to the claustrophobia of previous village life, but this speeding up of our lives has led to a craving for nostalgia and quirkiness. These opportunities, while enjoyable, can bring sterility to a village; tidying not enriching, demanding not giving, these are qualities that it is easy for a village to unthinkingly endorse.

The creeping development of suburbia is also scheduled to affect us. Many villages (like the fictitious Ambridge) are sufficiently far from nearby towns to avoid becoming part of their suburbs, but Clifford Chambers is not in that category. Stratford-upon-Avon has subsumed several nearby villages and a number of substantial new developments are either begun or under consideration in the ten miles around. In the last twenty years, the roads around Clifford Chambers have become wider and faster, and new roads create the opportunity for infill building. Sooner or later, Clifford Chambers will become a suburb of Stratford which could present the opportunity to reconsider its values.

We started this short concluding chapter by quoting Andrew Motion's assertion regarding the dysfunction between town and country living. This concern is increasingly widely felt; from cheerful television sitcom programmes such as *The Good Life* to recent books, articles and Internet reporting which reveal a trend in modern society to revisit the values of country living, not for the sake of nostalgia but from environmental concern.

Clifford Chambers has a fine set of allotments, not in the Square but tucked away on the other side of the main street. Chickens have made a comeback and bees are mooted. This will make no difference to the pace of climate change or to the suburbs of Stratford trailing down the B4632 or to the societal changes that will inevitably accompany such events, but it might help us survive them.

There is a story of an Anglo-Saxon noble who accepted Christianity and was about to be baptised when he said that he just had to check with the river god that such a step was acceptable. Perhaps those people had got it right, as they set up homes above the river-water flood-line on the land that is now the Square and the churchyard.

Call it Gaia or call it Arcadia or call it the strong brown river god, to 'worship' means to respect the worth of, and whether we respect the worth of this particular bit of land with enough intelligence and altruism, is the question we leave for the future to answer. ◎◎

A green man grotesque from the west exterior
wall of St St Helen's church
Probably early to mid fifteenth-century carving

The exhaust pipes of nearby cars were photographed as an illustration of the current residents' ubiquitous dependance on car usage

87

Sarah Hosking and John Cheal
in the door window of no.33

ACKNOWLEDGEMENTS AND PERMISSIONS

We wish to thank the Parish Council of Clifford Chambers and Milcote for permissions and the chairman, Stefan Buczacki for his contributed chapter 'The River' and his kind encouragement throughout two years' work on this project

Specific thanks are as follows:

'The River' by Stefan Buczacki

'This account has been written with sincere appreciation of the advice of many present and former Clifford residents, most notably Jim Adam and Christine Spratt; and also the inestimable help of the Environment Agency and Warwickshire County Archaeologist'.

'The Properties' by Nat Alcock

'I thank the people living in the Square who have kindly allowed me to visit their houses'.

The trustees of the HHT have given support and financial authorisation to this project but especial thanks are extended to Elizabeth Speller and to the Trust's chair, Revd Dr Paul Edmonson for his contributions and help

Grateful thanks are extended to neighbours in the Village who have allowed us to photograph their eyes, also their front doors and their car exhaust pipes and who have generously contributed pictures and provided reminiscences. Especial thanks are extended to Len and Lynne Moseley for access to the Village Archive, to the Wilks family for photographs of three generations of marriages, to Sally Abell for her supportive friendship and Charmian Evans for suggestions and for proof-reading the manuscript

Personal thanks are also extended to Andrew Holtom of Holtom Computer Services, to John Cheal (photographer) and the Stratford branch of Staples for their professional patience and help

Thanks are extended to Warwickshire County Record Office for permission to reproduce images from the Pippet Archive, to Warwickshire County Museums for permission to photograph items and reproduce those images and to Warwickshire County Council Geographic Information Systems

Thanks to the Shakespeare Birthplace Trust library and collections and to the Reich family

The quotation from *The Buildings of England: Warwickshire* by Nikolaus Pevsner is reproduced by kind permission of Yale University Press

'Church Going' by Philip Larkin and an extract from 'The Pike' by Ted Hughes are printed by permission of Faber and Faber

An extract from 'The River God' is printed by permission of the Stevie Smith Estate

'An Older England' by Felix Dennis (from *Tales from the Woods*, Ebury Press 2010) is printed by permission of Felix Dennis

'The Curfew Tolls' by Miles Burrows is printed by permission of the *Times Literary Supplement* and the author

The Portrait of Michael Drayton is reproduced by permission of the National Portrait Gallery

Financial support has been gratefully received from The Anson Charitable Trust, the Marc Fitch Fund and from two anonymous donors

We have made every effort to secure appropriate permissions and copyright clearance on the images and quotations included in this manuscript, and we regret any omissions remaining.